Titles already published

Alex de Waal, *AIDS and Power: Why There is No Political Crisis – Yet*

Tim Allen, *Trial Justice: The International Criminal Court and the Lord's Resistance Army*

Raymond W. Copson, *The United States in Africa*

Chris Alden, *China in Africa*

Tom Porteous, *Britain in Africa*

Julie Flint and Alex de Waal, *Darfur: A New History of a Long War*

Jonathan Glennie, *The Trouble with Aid: Why Less Could Mean More for Africa*

Peter Uvin, *Life after Violence: A People's Story of Burundi*

Bronwen Manby, *Struggles for Citizenship in Africa*

Camilla Toulmin, *Climate Change in Africa*

Orla Ryan, *Chocolate Nations: Living and Dying for Cocoa in West Africa*

Theodore Trefon, *Congo Masquerade: The Political Culture of Aid Inefficiency and Reform Failure*

Léonce Ndikumana and James Boyce, *Africa's Odious Debts: How Foreign Loans and Capital Flight Bled a Continent*

Mary Harper, *Getting Somalia Wrong? Faith, War and Hope in a Shattered State*

Neil Carrier and Gernot Klantschnig, *Africa and the War on Drugs*

Alcinda Honwana, *Youth and Revolution in Tunisia*

Marc Epprecht, *Sexuality and Social Justice in Africa: Rethinking Homosexuality and Forging Resistance*

Lorenzo Cotula, *The Great African Land Grab? Agricultural Investments and the Global Food System*

Michael Deibert, *The Democratic Republic of Congo: Between Hope and Despair*

Adam Branch and Zachariah Mampilly, *Africa Uprising: Popular Protest and Political Change*

Celeste Hicks, *Africa's New Oil: Power, Pipelines and Future Fortunes*

Forthcoming

Keith Breckenridge, *Mining, Power and Politics in South Africa: Rethinking the African Resource Curse*

Mick Moore, Odd-Helge Fjeldstad and Wilson Prichard, *Taxing Africa*

Kris Berwouts, *War and Failed Peace in Eastern Congo*

Theodore Trefon, *Congo's Environmental Paradox*

Published by Zed Books and the IAI with the support of the following organizations:

International African Institute The International African Institute's principal aim is to promote scholarly understanding of Africa, notably its changing societies, cultures and languages. Founded in 1926 and based in London, it supports a range of seminars and publications including the journal *Africa*.

www.internationalafricaninstitute.org

Royal African Society Now more than a hundred years old, the Royal African Society today is Britain's leading organization promoting Africa's cause. Through its journal, *African Affairs*, and by organizing meetings, discussions and other activities, the society strengthens links between Africa and Britain and encourages understanding of Africa and its relations with the rest of the world.

www.royalafricansociety.org

The World Peace Foundation, founded in 1910, is located at the Fletcher School, Tufts University. The Foundation's mission is to promote innovative research and teaching, believing that these are critical to the challenges of making peace around the world, and should go hand in hand with advocacy and practical engagement with the toughest issues. Its central theme is 'reinventing peace' for the twenty-first century.

www.worldpeacefoundation.org

About the author

Morten Jerven teaches at the School for International Studies at Simon Fraser University in Vancouver, Canada. He is the author of *Poor Numbers: How We Are Misled by African Development Statistics and What to Do About It*, and has published widely on African economic development, especially on patterns of economic growth and economic development statistics.

MORTEN JERVEN

AFRICA

Why economists get it wrong

Zed Books
LONDON

in association with

International African Institute
Royal African Society
World Peace Foundation

Africa: Why economists get it wrong was first published in association with the International African Institute, the Royal African Society and the World Peace Foundation in 2015 by Zed Books Ltd, Unit 2.8, The Foundry, 17 Oval Way, London SE11 5RR, UK

www.zedbooks.co.uk
www.internationalafricaninstitute.org
www.royalafricansociety.org
www.worldpeacefoundation.org

Set in OurType Arnhem and Futura Bold by Ewan Smith, London
Index: <ed.emery@thefreeuniversity.net>
Cover designed by www.roguefour.co.uk

ISBN 978-1-78360-133-2 hb
ISBN 978-1-78360-132-5 pb
ISBN 978-1-78360-134-9 pdf
ISBN 978-1-78360-135-6 epub
ISBN 978-1-78360-136-3 mobi

Contents

Tables and figures

Acknowledgments

I have been researching patterns of economic growth in sub-Saharan Africa since I was an MSc student and later a PhD student in economic history at the London School of Economics and Political Science (LSE). During that decade I have received more advice and feedback than I can recount here. I am grateful to the editors at Zed Books and the International African Institute, Ken Barlow and Stephanie Kitchen and the rest of the editorial board, for believing in this book project, and to staff at the Royal African Society and *African Arguments* for their willing assistance in planning this book.

This is a distilled version of the work I have published on growth in African economies during the past five years. Longer and more technical versions of parts of the arguments I put forward here have been tested and tried in research and review articles published by the *Journal of African Economies*, *Journal of Development Studies*, *Journal of International Development*, *African Affairs*, *Economic History Review* and *Economic History of Development Regions*. I am grateful to the editors of these journals and, of course, to the anonymous reviewers for comments on my manuscript. Finally, and in particular with regards to Chapter 4, I am grateful for the support from scholars and officials I have worked with in Africa and the rest of the world on my quest for transparency surrounding the procedures that generate data on African growth, poverty and development.

Finally, I am most indebted to my loved ones. This book is dedicated to my little ones William and Robin, and my remarkable wife Taraneh.

Introduction

For the past two decades, mainstream economists who study African economic growth have been trying to explain something that never happened (Mkandawire and Soludo 1999). Economists have focused almost exclusively on one question: why has economic growth failed in Africa? This perspective has made its way into popular domains. Most famously, in 2000, the front page of *The Economist* depicted Africa as a hopeless continent that was unable to experience economic growth and development. In a special report on the continent, the magazine asked: 'Does Africa have some inherent character flaw that keeps it backward and incapable of development?' (*Economist* 2000).

Yet only eleven years later, *The Economist* had a completely different front-page report about Africa as a hopeful continent that was on the rise (*Economist* 2011). How could they have got it so wrong the first time? In 2000, Johannesburg's weekly business magazine *Financial Mail* pointed out that, in 1997, just three years earlier, *The Economist* had written that 'sub-Saharan Africa is in better shape than it has been for a generation'. The *Financial Mail* asked: 'Do the editors of *The Economist* have a character flaw that makes them incapable of consistent judgment?'[1]

As Bob Dylan told us, you do not need a weatherman to tell you which way the wind blows.[2] *The Economist* is just a popular news-reporting magazine, so one should perhaps not be too surprised that its judgment varies and turns with the current. In the year 2000, the editors were looking back at two decades of news stories from Africa that focused on famines, civil wars and failure. The magazine's perspective in 2000 was very much a child of its own time. However, it was a rash evaluation that ignored certain fundamentals in African economic development.

However, from the 'weathermen' in the story of Africa's development – actual economists – one would expect an opinion that relies on long-term patterns and history and stands the test of time. Yet, as this book shows, economists continue to get Africa wrong. How wrong – and why they keep getting economic growth in Africa wrong – is the topic of this book.

When the editors at *The Economist* declared that Africa was hopeless, they were not just putting their finger in the air to see which way the wind was blowing, they were taking inspiration from the consensus in the economic literature at the time. Since the 1990s, almost all economic studies of Africa had focused on explaining why there had been a 'chronic failure of growth' on that continent. In 1999, Paul Collier and Jan Wilhelm Gunning wrote an article summarizing the consensus in the mainstream economic literature after a decade of research that sought to explain economic growth in Africa. At the time, they said: 'It is clear that Africa has suffered a chronic failure of economic growth. The problem for analysis is to determine its causes' (Collier and Gunning 1999b: 4).

That was written in 1999, but, even more strikingly, in 2007 Paul Collier wrote in much the same vein. He identified the 'Bottom Billion', the population of the world that (according to Collier) live in countries that do not experience economic growth. He identified just under 60 countries that he calls Africa+.[3] In his assessment, 'The central problem of the "Bottom Billion" is that they have not grown. The failure of the growth process in these societies simply has to be our core concern, and curing it the core challenge of development' (Collier 2007: 11).

Collier explained how African economies have been caught in four different poverty traps: the conflict trap; the natural resource trap; the trap of being landlocked with bad neighbors; and, finally, the trap of bad governance in a small country. These problems are what makes these countries incapable of growth (ibid.). In retrospect, what is so striking is that this statement was made just after a period of rapid economic growth since the mid-1990s in the very economies Collier was talking about. The majority of the economies that Collier described as chronic failures had been growing for more than a decade. Many countries grew before, after and even during the time when Collier was writing his book. The empirical evidence for the existence of such poverty traps is in fact weak, but the power of the metaphor and the catchiness of the phrase 'Bottom Billion' meant that the misleading notion of a chronic failure in Africa lived on, way past its due date.

In 2014, after more than ten years of growth in most African economies, some economists have finally begun to recognize the change (Miguel 2009). My book starts by asking why it took so long for economists to recognize that African economies were growing again. The other central question I examine is why economists missed the fact that

African economies were growing before the 1990s. Most datasets will tell you that many African economies grew rapidly in the 1950s, the 1960s, and even into the 1970s. However, in their overwhelming focus on explaining why African economies failed, economists and others lost track of the gains these economies made in the initial period after independence. Why has mainstream economics found it so easy to ignore these growth patterns? I argue that this is because the models economists use are fundamentally ahistorical.

The notion of the 'African growth tragedy' is very time specific (Easterly and Levine 1997; see also Easterly 2001a). It was born in the late 1990s, as economists looked back at the period since the mid-1970s. Today, after more than a decade when growth has again been the rule – not the exception – it seems exceedingly unsuitable to use those two 'lost decades' as the defining period of African development capacity. Yet the current growth literature recycles this misrepresentation of economic growth; the emphasis has not been on explaining economic performance but rather on finding factors that can explain the total income differential in gross domestic product (GDP) per capita between countries today.

Daron Acemoglu and James Robinson have recently offered a grand explanation of why nations fail (2012). This work is not interested in explaining economic growth; they are interested in explaining the difference in income levels between nations today. Their focus is on finding root causes for why some countries have failed. So rather than explaining why, for example, the economy of Tanzania grew each year by 1 percent from 1960 to 1990 while the economy of Japan grew at 4 percent,[4] they instead look at variables that can explain the difference in GDP per capita between, say, $1,000 in Tanzania and $20,000 in Japan in the year 2000. They propose that the cause of the $19,000 difference is that Tanzania was exposed to colonial rule and inherited 'bad' institutions, whereas Japan was not exposed to the 'wrong' type of colonial rule and therefore economic prosperity has been assured by its 'good' institutions. For Tanzanians, the difference between $500 and $1,000 is more relevant, and the main target for Tanzanians should be how to get to $2,000 or otherwise experience a sustained and significant improvement in living standards.

It is not only useless to discover that the difference between Tanzania and Japan can be explained with econometrics by referring to a variable that captures ethnic fragmentation, quality of governance

3

or geographical location, it is also based on poor social science. In this book, I show how this poor scholarly practice has meant that the economic growth literature has misunderstood growth in Africa.

From explaining slow growth to explaining low income

This book documents how the mainstream growth literature has misunderstood the growth performance of sub-Saharan Africa in the postcolonial era. Chapter 1 looks at why the economic growth literature has focused on explaining a chronic failure of growth – something that never happened. What I call the first generation of economic growth literature – cross-country growth regressions from the early 1990s onward – looked for variables that measured economic policies that could be correlated statistically with low average growth in sub-Saharan Africa.

This 'first-generation' economic growth literature made several key mistakes. First, the analysis ignored changes in economic growth during the postcolonial period. Second, the variables that were supposed to capture what was called 'bad' policy were poorly identified and were largely observations taken from the 1980s. Thus, the economic growth literature mistakenly identified what were really the *effects* of an economic downturn as the *causes* of an economic downturn.

But the misunderstandings did not stop there, and instead of being corrected, these errors created the foundation for a second generation of growth literature – cross-country growth regressions from the early 2000s onward. The conclusion from the first generation of growth literature was that there was a chronic failure of growth in Africa. Thus, the next logical step was that there was no growth to explain and that what needed to be explained was the static gap in income between African economies and those of much of the rest of the world. A new literature arose that looked for correlates of low income. Moreover, for technical reasons I will explain in Chapter 2, the literature looked to history for such variables. I discuss how this new regression literature, while arguing that 'history matters' for economic development, has used a method of investigation that is ahistorical.

In order to understand the effect of externally driven growth, Chapter 3 discusses lessons from previous shocks and booms in African economies and puts forward the idea that we need to focus less on aggregate growth and more on the political economy of growth, asking who benefits. The chapter discusses the recent period of growth in Africa and the prospects for future growth. In place of the current mainstream explanation, I suggest an alternative explanation for economic growth in African economies. I demonstrate how most African economies grew from the 1950s to the 1970s and then contracted with a debt crisis and other shocks in the 1970s. Lessons from history are crucial for understanding and managing the current period of economic growth in sub-Saharan Africa. I show that growth in Africa has been a recurring process. Understanding African economies is not just a matter of getting the history right: the policy implications of fluctuating growth and institutional change are radically different from the implications drawn from theories of chronic growth and static institutions.

In Chapter 4, I discuss a problem that the mainstream economic literature has ignored: the quality of the statistics on which economists rely.[5] All mainstream economic analysis of economic growth relies on data that correlate economic growth, measured as GDP per capita, with other variables such as inflation, malaria prevalence, democratic elections or distance from London. Economists have created models in which high growth or high GDP per capita is correlated with low inflation, low rates of malaria, many elections and closeness to London – on average. That is the gist of the analysis. Surprisingly perhaps, the quality of the underlying data has not been well examined. In Chapter 4, I review some of the problems but I also ask a fundamental question: what should we think of the most recent growth in Africa? Is Africa's rise real? Since the 1990s, the GDPs of many small countries in Africa have been increasing at a high rate. A portion of these increases is a statistical fiction and a portion represents genuine progress. However, GDP numbers tell us too little about what has really happened or about whether living conditions on the African continent are improving.

I argue that it would be wrong to celebrate the recent growth as a triumph of economic and political liberalization. Growth in Africa is to some extent old news – recurring growth has happened because of Africa's long-term pattern of exporting natural resources – and the region now depends more than ever before on external demand for its sustained economic growth. The conclusion discusses the policy implications of an analysis that approaches African economies as experiencing recurring growth instead of seeing them as examples of failed growth and looks at the extent to which the history of economic growth is a guide for future growth.

5

How economists have misunderstood growth in Africa

The overarching question in the economic growth literature has been about why Africa has grown relatively slowly. This question has over-shadowed other more important questions, such as howAfrican econ-omies have grown. If the question had been about how African economies are developing, there would have been more to explain and the literature could have given policy makers something useful to work with. Unfor-tunately, that question was not asked.

We currently have an economic growth literature that explains why bad policies mean that there is no growth in Africa. The trouble with this model is that the current explanation problem is not one of a lack of growth but rather of how to interpret rapid economic growth. With the help of the historical datasets on slaves, colonial settlers and linguistic mapping, economists have been able to find different variables that can explain why African states have 'bad' institutions, have failed and are stuck in zero-growth traps. The difficulty with this analysis is that, despite all their shortcomings and despite all their institutional differences from their European counterparts, African states have experienced periods of economic growth.

The fact that mainstream economics continues to get this wrong is of great importance. This is not just an academic disagreement. International financial institutions such as the World Bank and the In-ternational Monetary Fund (IMF) give economic models and economists a central role in the decisions they make. Because of this, economists' mistakes spill into the policy world. Indeed, the story of how economists explain economic growth in Africa is strongly linked to the history of policy making in Africa, and particularly to the role of external policy advice and policy directives.

The question 'Why is Africa growing slowly?' appeared in the late 1970s and the early 1980s. The most influential answer was given in what is known as the Berg report,[6] a World Bank report that firmly placed the blame for slow growth in Africa with African policy makers. According to the report, African states intervened too much in mar-kets, gave too low a priority to agriculture, and otherwise pursued misguided policies. The economic growth literature, as we will see, went to considerable lengths to affirm this orthodoxy, and, despite empirical evidence to the contrary, has managed to present a history of African economic growth that finds a correlation between 'bad' policy – defined as state intervention in markets – and slow growth.

The literature has thereby provided empirical 'proof' that the mainstream diagnosis and prescription for poor countries were correct and that there was a relationship between 'good' policy – as embodied in the liberalization package termed the 'Washington Consensus' – and positive economic performance.[7]

Yet the economic record tells us rather clearly that the liberalization policies of the 1990s failed in many ways, and that state intervention in the 1960s and 1970s was not always catastrophic. It is important to remember that state intervention does not always equate to states suppressing markets. Sometimes states substitute for nonexistent markets or they nudge economic actors to engage in markets. Therefore, liberalizing agricultural marketing simply by closing down a state-run agricultural marketing board does not mean that a free and fair market that organizes fertilizer, seeds, advances, purchases, transportation, forecasting and information will suddenly appear. It is not safe to assume that this will happen. Economic growth did not revive after liberalization policies were implemented. Instead, the economic – and particularly the political – crisis deepened and arguably persisted for two decades (Easterly 2001c; van de Walle 2001).

Instead of engaging in a wholesale reconsideration of the diagnosis made in the 1990s, with its emphasis on 'good' policies and the market mantra of 'getting the prices right', the economics literature shifted its focus in the 2000s. In the second-generation growth literature, the emphasis of scholarly work changed from investigating relations between policy and growth to linking current development outcomes with historical events such as colonialism and the slave trade. Instead of introspection about whether 'bad' policy was actually to blame for slow economic growth, some economists determined that advising 'good' policy was not enough. The root cause was not 'bad policy', it was 'bad governance' and 'poor institutions'.

The second-generation growth literature focused on policy makers and policy implementation as the sources of the problem with economic growth. The refrain that it was 'getting the prices right' that mattered changed: now governance and institutions mattered. This is when the idea that some places were destined to fail at development was born, and this provided the foundation for the question and the answer in *The Economist* ten years ago. Do African states have a character flaw that makes them incapable of development? 'Yes,' said *The Economist* (and the economists on whom the magazine relied).

7

But while that analysis coheres well with the consensus in the economic literature, it does not match what is going on in the economies concerned. Some even say that Africa is rising. This book shows that there is nothing surprising or new about that.

This emphasis on finding what was wrong with the history and politics of Africa meant that 'Africa' itself was launched as an explanatory category (see, for instance, Ferguson 2007). Mkandawire captured the absurdity of the situation in his inaugural lecture as Chair of African Development at the London School of Economics and Political Science (2011: 2): 'The name of the Chair – African Development – is something of an oxymoron, and as bewildering a possibility in development studies as the bumblebee is in aerodynamics.'

African states were misdiagnosed and dismissed as being incapable of development based on observations made during the 1980s and early 1990s, a period when most African economies were experiencing the deepest recession of the twentieth century. The characteristics they exhibited during this period were not representative of longer trajectories. It is true that most states have not been perfectly efficient for the past five decades, but it is equally evident that their dealings have not been perfectly disastrous either. Herein lies the crucial error of comparison. The verdict about the quality of these states, or 'governance', was made by comparing actual states in the Africa of the 1980s with idealized, perfectly functioning states that do not exist (Mkandawire 2001; Kelsall 2013). While it is true that African states have fallen short of these kinds of expectations, such comparisons have not told us how serious these relative shortcomings have been in terms of economic growth.

My message is quite simple. We need to rephrase the central research question about African economic growth. The question is not 'Why has Africa failed?' but 'Why did African economies grow and then decline only to grow again?' It is important to get the history of economic growth in Africa right, but perhaps it is more important to know that the *right* history fundamentally changes the policy implications for future growth on the African continent. The pessimism about policies and institutions in Africa has been overstated. In most cases, a wholesale change of institutions or governance is not necessary for economic growth.

So that's the argument. Economic analysis has painted an overly dismal picture of the African growth record. Growth in Africa has been misunderstood, and as a result the discipline of economics is currently unable to give useful policy advice, let alone simply explain what is happening right now. In the following chapters I show how this came to be the case. It is the result of a very particular method and the use of very particular evidence: a method that relies on correlations in country-level datasets. The method and evidence limit what kind of questions can be asked and the answers are weakened by the quality of the evidence. The analysis is drawn from an observation of static averages instead of a historical investigation of economic change and the evolution of political institutions.

Non-specialist and non-economist audiences are often persuaded by the rhetorical power of economics (McCloskey 1998); however, when we look closer and start questioning assumptions, about the underlying theory or model of change and about the quality of the numbers used in the investigation, the central findings of the economics literature on Africa look far more contestable (Jerven 2013c). I do not think that all economists get everything wrong about Africa all the time. Many economists do good work on Africa, uncovering new evidence and posing interesting research questions. And, of course, some of the critiques put forward here rely on work done by economists. Economists are not a homogeneous group, and some are more worried than others about the limits of the methods and evidence in their empirical work. William Easterly, for instance, probably gave Paul Collier the most scathing review:[8]

> Valid statistical results must meet stringent conditions. The usual standard for labeling a result 'significant' is that it could have occurred by chance only one out of twenty times, assuming a statistical exercise is run only once. An unfortunately all-too-common practice called 'data mining' involves running twenty statistical exercises and then reporting only the one that produces a 'significant' result (which will have happened by chance) (Easterly 2009).

There are, however, many practitioners of 'cookbook econometrics'[9] – those who just follow a recipe when they do so-called empirical work, running tests with downloaded datasets. There are also economists who are well aware of the weakness in their work but are often not very eager to clearly communicate the caveats in more popular domains, whereas in the original research papers such caveats are carefully subjected to footnote treatment. Moreover, the results of the statistical test are not all that convincing, and often economists then make use of anecdotes to persuade readers to believe the fragile evidence that is presented, as McGovern noted (2011: 353):

> I am struck by the extent to which economists, at least when they are writing about poor people in out of the way places, seem to rely on half-baked ethnographic insights, the kinds gleaned from corridor talk at meetings and by talking with taxi drivers on the way in from the airport and bartenders in business-class hotels.

It is beyond doubt that mainstream economics has a proven superiority in terms of providing influential 'numbers, patterns and stories' to the development community (ibid.).[10] How can and should non-economists engage with mainstream economics? How can the non-specialist contest an argument that is supported by advanced econometric methods? This book provides guidance. It invites readers to question the evidence, to interrogate the assumptions and to judge for themselves whether they think that the story the economic model tells us is a plausible one, and whether the policy implications derived from it are useful.

Is my criticism of economists fair? It is even-handed in the sense that it matches the impact economics has had on narratives about economic development in Africa and the self-assuredness with which many economists deliver their message. It is unfair in the sense that there are many economists who do useful analysis and contribute to our common endeavor of understanding economic growth and development better. I think that, in order to reach a better understanding, a bit more humility among many economists would be useful; in particular, a better understanding of the limits of their own datasets and statistical testing is needed. Indeed, it is striking to read books by economists who seem to argue that the problem with the world is that the world has thus far not followed their expert insights, whereas another plausible reading of the history of economic development is that such expert insights have systematically been wrong. As McGovern notes (ibid.: 347):

> the self-assuredness of economists such as Collier may be a part of the problem and not, as they suppose, a part of the solution. For an outsider, the strangest thing about the field of economics is the fact that although it appears to be wrong much of the time, rather than becoming chastened and introverted, most of its practitioners seem to become bolder, drawing strength from their failures.

We should not expect any major change of mind anytime soon, it seems. So, in the meantime, non-economists need better critical tools when reading economics.

Today, non-economists are most often exposed to the works of economists in best-selling books that present a narrative written for a popular readership, summarizing a range of papers previously published for a scholarly audience. These books may be a quick and easy way of catching up with what economists are saying, but they are – to varying degrees – principally designed to sell the arguments. If we want to see how these findings were reached, what was in the dataset, what assumptions were made, and how one might come up with equally satisfactory yet competing explanations, we have to dig into the underlying journal articles. This type of reading of economics helps students understand the methods of economists: that is, exposing 'how they come to know'. I hope that this book can help reshape some of the central research questions in the literature on African economic development and that it will guide readers in engaging with the economics literature critically.

1 | Misunderstanding economic growth in Africa

For two decades, mainstream economists studying African economic growth have been trying to explain a chronic failure of growth – something that never occurred (Mkandawire and Soludo 1999). I will explain how that could happen. I will also show how that attempt affects our ability to understand economic growth in Africa today. The work of economists is always evolving over time due to changes in methodology, theory and technology (Morgan 2012). In the 1980s, some important innovations took place that had significant implications for the scholarly work of economists. The first step was a gradual tendency away from theorizing about economic growth toward conducting empirical tests of growth theory.[1] As we will see, it is one thing to think about what the factors that determine economic growth might be, but it is quite another to use real-world data from all the countries of the globe in order to test whether the theory of what drives economic growth holds.

Theoretically, the basics of economic growth are straightforward and self-explanatory. The factors that drive economic growth – called the factors of production – are labor, land and capital. Together, these three factors produce goods and services. Economic growth is therefore a result of the increased use of the factors of production. Output increases when more people, more capital or more land is used for production.

Although this is called economic growth, it is a particular kind of economic growth known as extensive growth. In extensive growth, you only get more for more: that is, the increases in economic growth are proportional, or less than proportional, to increases in the use of resources. Intensive growth is what happens when growth is more than the proportional increases in the factors of production. Any growth that is not attributable to the increased use of resources is often referred to as 'total factor productivity' in the growth literature. The total factor productivity increase can be a result of improving the quality of the inputs. And this is often interpreted as technology – which has a broad definition and ranges from things such as smart gadgets to general changes in how production is organized to legal frameworks and structures in society at large (Jones 1988).

For an intuitive way of understanding why output may be increasing more than would be proportional to the increase in inputs, I use the example of moving a sofa. If you are one person trying to move your own sofa, productivity is very low. It is hard to get a grip on the sofa. If you get help from your friend (or you add one more unit of labor), total productivity more than doubles. If you add another friend, there is no increase in productivity; there may even be a decrease in output, as your second friend might distract you, order pizza or otherwise get in your way when you are trying to move the sofa. Productivity could also benefit from capital investment technology (such as using a strap, putting the sofa on a trolley, or using a forklift or a van). Such increases in output would require both capital and technology, and they would only be justified if you were in the business of moving many sofas regularly. Thus, there is more than one way of increasing output – some comes through adding more input/s and some through improved methods and technology – and the relationship between outputs and inputs is not linear, nor is it always rational to maximize output.

The bottom line is that economic growth goes far beyond mere increments of labor and capital. The sources and determinants of economic growth are not limited to basic processes of accumulation. How production is organized matters, and this extends to the very fabric of society – the rules that govern human behavior, or what economists have become accustomed to referring to as 'institutions' (see Bardhan 2005). We can understand this, but to go ahead and use data on labor, capital and GDP growth and then empirically measure it is quite another matter.

Initially, economists were quite happy to leave total factor productivity as an unexplained residual. In a framework called 'growth accounting', you enter increments in capital or labor as explanatory or independent variables in a system of equations that explain changes in economic growth. By doing this, you can, with a few assumptions, calculate how much of the economic growth is accounted for by labor and capital and how much of that growth is total factor productivity (Crafts 2002).

While early growth models did not seek to explain different rates of total factor productivity, this changed with a move toward models of economic growth in which total factor productivity was explained within the model, or endogenously. The turning point is best illustrated by what is called the Lucas paradox. In a famous journal article, Lucas posed the question: 'Why doesn't capital flow from rich to poor countries?' (Lucas 1990). The article presented the basic tenets of 'new' growth theory. According to the standard assumptions of neoclassical growth theory, India should have had 50 times more investment than it had received and it should have joined the richest economies in the world. Since this had not happened, Lucas suggested that maybe something was missing from the old exogenous growth models and proposed a new *endogenous* model. In the new model, variables that captured policies and other features of the economy were added to the basic factors of production as determinants of economic growth.

Thus, the theoretical growth literature went from focusing solely on rates of capital accumulation to emphasizing human capital and other country-specific characteristics that determine differences in country-level growth. This development has continued to the present; economists today think that growth is determined by institutions and historical events. We will see that this change in thinking about economic growth was not driven by theoretical considerations alone. The literature evolved through a process of empirical trial and error, technological and methodological innovation, and the availability of new datasets. In the 1980s and 1990s, more global datasets on economic growth, education levels and other variables became available, and, equipped with greater computing power and new models of economic growth to fit the new tools, the work of growth economists became concerned with running regressions and looking for correlations between datasets. Thus, we went from heroically making assumptions about the uniformity of economic activity and stability of returns across time to hoping that we could say something about the relative importance of increments in labor and capital in accounting for increases in output, and then to a much braver approach of hoping that we could say something about the *causes* of economic growth. Wording shifted from talking about accounting for growth and correlates of growth toward the more ambitious determinants of growth – and finally to the causes of growth. It is clear to any economists that this is a messy job, but just how messy is not communicated clearly. Before we proceed to lay bare this process of scholarly innovation to solve the African growth puzzle, we should go through some of the basic pitfalls of statistical testing – particularly that of looking at correlates in datasets.

Correlation is not causation

It would be difficult to think of a truism that is more often repeated and is so frequently violated in the social sciences. The contribution of mainstream economists to the study of poor economies and their politics is fundamentally based on observing country characteristics on the one hand and indicators that describe levels of development on the other. In a regression analysis, one is assumed to explain the other. This is the leap of faith from correlation to causation, and, for various reasons, mistakenly taking this leap has led economists astray in the elusive quest to explain growth in poor economies.

Since the 1990s, the bread and butter work of growth economists has consisted of running different datasets against each other in cross-country regressions and searching for a publishable result that proves or tests a hypothesis of economic development. There is nothing wrong with empirical testing. In fact, it should be encouraged. The problem arises when the testing is not guided by theory.

As an example, I tend to use the myth that storks bring babies. It is obvious to those of us who have an understanding of how babies are made that these little wonders do not make it into this world thanks to the ministrations of storks. This runs contrary to the explanation given to young children in folklore and in modern cartoons (such as Disney's movie *Dumbo*). So where does this hypothesis of storks bringing babies come from? The stork and baby myth is a very convenient explanation based on a deliberately misinterpreted correlation.

For the origin of the myth we need to go back to the time before electric lights and industrialized societies emerged in northern Europe. When it got darker and darker in the months following the equinox, and as the harvest had been completed and animals brought home from summer pastures, there was less work to do outside and more leisure time inside. People spent most of their leisure time in dark houses covered by blankets to keep warm. Enough said. For many, this transition meant that little babies emerged nine months later, about the time when spring came – and this coincided with the storks returning from southern countries. And there you have it: a misguided theory was born to explain how babies arrived.

The lesson of this example is that correlation is not causation. If you run the datasets of stork arrivals against baby births, there is a significant positive relationship.[2] This abstract manner of conducting empirical research would indeed find a relationship between storks and babies. However, because such an investigation would not be grounded in a basic theoretical understanding of how babies come into this world, the researcher would still be a long way from unearthing the causal mechanisms. It is more than likely that he or she would draw the wrong type of policy advice from the research findings. Intriguingly, the arrival of babies and storks are linked. The researcher has found a real-world pattern but has failed to understand the relationship. Based on the investigation, the researcher might construct a model that suggests that, in order to reduce fertility in Denmark in the nineteenth century, policy makers should have focused their efforts on reducing the migration of storks. The scheme would have been expensive and misguided and, quite obviously, would not have had its intended effect. Conducting blind empirical tests by running different datasets against each other will lead researchers and policy makers astray.

Garbage in, garbage out

It is equally important to understand that the *quality* of the observations in the dataset matters. If you ask an economist about the evidence supporting their conclusions, they will direct you to the inferential statistical results and tell you about coefficients of determination, statistical significance and robustness tests. By contrast, if you ask a historian about evidence, he or she will respond by telling you about the quality of the primary observations.

This is a key difference. In my previous book on African development statistics, I pointed out a gap in our knowledge (Jerven 2013b). Since the arrival of global datasets on economic growth, poverty, politics and other variables, there has been surprisingly little questioning of the quality of the underlying observations. In some fields, such as the quantitative study of the correlates of war, there has been more probing of the quality of the different datasets (Cramer 2006); however, in the study of economics, there has been a tendency to take these datasets as 'facts'. The problem is that these data are not data in the literal meaning of the word – something that is given. Instead, they are often actively created and coded observations.

The standard defense of inferential statistics is that garbage in the dataset will bias the results toward zero. In statistics, one talks of this as false negatives and false positives. The easiest example is pregnancy. If you are declared not pregnant when you really are pregnant, that is a false negative. The false positive would be to state that you are pregnant when you are not. In the case of messy data, if one finds no relationship, it is often interpreted as finding that 'a' does not cause 'b'. Many zero results, which could be false negatives – such as finding that there is no relationship between development aid and economic growth – have been dominating the debates on economic development for more than a decade now (Easterly 2006). But that might be because data on both aid and growth are bad. The right answer is that we do not know because we cannot trust the data. So garbage data do matter, and they determine how we understand central questions in economic development.

Even more problems appear if there are systematic errors (as opposed to random errors) in the data. This happens all the time. In datasets with economic variables, there is often a tendency to understate production in certain sectors or to overstate poverty in particular areas. This problem becomes even more important with what are often called subjective datasets. These kinds of datasets are collections of opinions and responses to standardized questions. A classic example can be found in datasets on corruption. There are few direct observations and therefore very few systematic data on corruption (Aidt 2009), so instead the most commonly used datasets on corruption are a selection of opinion surveys: someone calls up businesspeople and asks them how corrupt country Y is on a scale from one to ten. Do you think that Swedes might understate the level of corruption in Sweden and that foreign businessmen might overstate corruption in Nigeria? This is how these subjective datasets are collected and it means that a large amount of literature built on correlations between corruption and growth is standing on very shaky foundations.[3]

It is not just potential systematic errors that result from using subjective metrics in the datasets. It might also be that the datasets are not suitable for testing because the measures for corruption do not assess actual levels of corruption but rather they give an overall opinion of the efficiency of the economic and political system at a very specific point in time. That means that the endogeneity problem – or reversal causality – is built into the datasets from the outset.

Let us say that you conducted a survey of the quality of governance in Malawi in the fall of 2010.[4] At that time, the country was experiencing several interruptions to its petroleum supply (and therefore also to the provision of electricity and the transportation of goods and people). This was because of temporary balance-of-payment problems.

In a survey of visitors to Malawi that month, you would get results that ranked Malawi very poorly with regard to the quality of institutions compared with the evaluations you might collect in a month or year when there were no such interruptions. Yet the leadership and the set of policies in place during the alternative time frame may be the same. In the hands of the economist, this dataset enters the field of growth regressions, and what was really just a snapshot of a complex picture turns into a very specific causal story where 'poor economic governance' caused 'slow growth'. Meanwhile, we have learned nothing at all about the role played by the quality of institutions during this temporary shortfall in imports, about how the quality of institutions related to slow growth, or about what the actual physical and political causes of the shortfall were.[5]

Errors attached to the numbers used in the economic growth literature are indeed often systematic, and thus we may have serious measurement bias, particularly when approaching policy questions in poor countries. Whether the end result is that the analysis finds no relationship or that it finds the wrong relationship, the outcome is unsatisfactory. Poor numbers will mislead us.

One of the most innovative areas of economic research is the one that comes up with 'proxies' to measure phenomena that are not easily quantified or observed. A particularly telling example comes from India, in a paper by Besley and Burgess (2000) investigating the effect of land reform on poverty. A priori, there are good reasons to think that redistributive land reform (taking property from the rich and giving it to the poor) might reduce poverty. But can it be measured? Poverty might be poorly measured, but with land reform it is even harder. A lot of land legislation was passed in India, but, as any purveyor of Indian rural agrarian history knows, those who had land were very resistant to distributing it. A good historian or a good ethnographer could answer this question by sifting through archives for documents proving that land shifted hands, or by using interviews to map land change over time. For the macroeconomist, this is unnecessary. The authors instead used the total number of land reforms undertaken as a proxy for land distribution and checked whether the number of land reforms in a state was correlated with poverty decline. They found some evidence of a link, but you would have to be willing to take a leap of faith to accept the results. Arguably, the authors provided a mathematically precise answer to the wrong question. We already think that there is a relationship between pro-poor land reform and reduced poverty. What we might have wanted to know is what kind of land reform actually causes land to change hands.[6]

As will be documented here, using proxies may indeed be a smart shortcut. Almost all conversation depends on letting something stand in for something else. The danger is that, while we are letting proxies stand in for real observations, we may forget this when we interpret the results. Proving causality with cross-country correlations in macro-variables is already messy – but if we let 'assassinations' be used as a proxy for political stability, or 'elections held' a proxy for the quality of institutions, we may gradually lose sight of the levels of abstractions.

Perhaps the most frequently overlooked problem is missing data – or things that are uncounted or unrecorded. Generally, there are more data about what crosses international borders, more records of goods that were marketed through official channels, and better coverage of large-scale economic activities in urban centers, while datasets sometimes contain no information at all about domestic exchange, household consumption or small-scale economic activities in rural areas. The history of colonial Africa, for instance, usually gives undue space, if not undue emphasis, to the role of colonial administrators because written sources and quantitative evidence about that topic is available.

Because of their need for quantitative evidence to test their models, for econometricians and cliometricians datasets are in effect the boundary of investigation (Jerven 2011a; 2012a). It is quite obvious that not all that can be counted counts and not all that counts is counted.[7] But the impact of missing data on scholarly analysis is not usually appreciated fully. Because of the availability (or unavailability) of evidence, our investigations are biased – and this means that scholars write very specific political and economic histories. Of course, this is a general point to make about any social science endeavor, but in the study of Africa and its economic history it is perhaps one of the most important observations (Parker and Rathbone 2007). The unevenness of the availability of both current and historical data may skew accounts of economic change.

The unevenness of available data affects knowledge production in two specific ways. First, there are major blind spots. In African economic histories that have been written using time series data about economic growth, year 1 has been 1960. That is, of course, an artificial starting point, but data availability determines what kinds of questions and what time frames can be investigated. These data limitations determine the narratives that can be told.

A striking example of the power of datasets and the importance of the vantage point comes from the debate on global warming. It took a long time for anyone to notice global warming because of weaknesses in the global mean temperature dataset (Maslin 2004: 27). In the 1970s, the data series went back only a few decades, and from that particular viewpoint it looked as if temperatures had been falling since the 1940s. But the current dataset, which covers the period 1860–2010, shows that the temperatures are indeed on an increasing trend.

When you do not have a complete picture, your impression may be biased. Every cross-country growth regression starts with the goal of using a global sample, but because of incomplete data availability, some countries are excluded from the equations. The assumption that a country's lack of ability or opportunity to conduct a household survey is not correlated with any other determinants of poverty or slow growth is a brave one. Continent-wide statements on recent economic growth and trends in poverty are based on observations from a small subset of the world's nations. Sometimes the missing observations are 'made up' for some countries by the international organizations that fill in the gaps when datasets are assembled; at other times economists extrapolate data from neighboring countries to produce data for a country that has no data to contribute (Jerven 2013b: 8–32).[8]

These are key weaknesses in the data, and they shape how growth in Africa is explained. Data are missing from some countries, and, for most economists, the story of growth starts in 1960. GDP data record some decline in growth in the formal sector, but fail to capture economic change in the *informal* sector. Perhaps most importantly, for many of the concepts that we think are theoretically related to economic growth – concepts such as 'policies' and 'institutions' – there are no direct quantitative data. Instead, different survey rankings, subjective metrics and various proxies are used to capture the effects of 'policies' and 'institutions'. This process of matching growth data with metrics of other phenomena is what I will explore as I turn to growth, correlates of growth, and the story of mainstream economics' attempts to explain growth in Africa.

The African dummy variable

The starting point for what I have called 'the quest for the African dummy' is arguably a 1991 article by Robert J. Barro (Jerven 2011c). His essay exploring the causes of economic growth in a global sample of countries provided the template for the next decade of research on economic growth.[9] This investigation was made possible by the availability of global datasets on economic growth, such as the Penn World Tables, the arrival of which was considered to be 'an important statistical event' that expanded the boundary of empirical research (Stern 1989: 600).[10] The boundaries of historical investigation for development economists were effectively set by these datasets; for instance, Paul Collier wrote in 1993: 'Africa offers the imminent prospect to applied macroeconomics of perhaps thirty national time series data sets' (1993: 60). The datasets offered economists unprecedented freedom to test relationships between those sets, although some did still lack a number of observations: 'Perhaps the main obstacle to understanding growth is the small number of countries in the world' (Durlauf et al. 2005: 558).

The combination of a new methodology and new data sources spurred a great amount of research. The articles and essays this research generated used the methodology of cross-country growth regressions in which the dependent variable was the average growth rate of per capita GDP. Researchers added different independent variables, or interactions of independent variables, to the initial baseline estimation in their search for new insights about what correlates with economic growth (ibid.: 599).

In cross-country regressions, the *dependent* variable is the variation in average GDP growth at the country level and also the variable that is to be explained. The *independent* variables are the things that explain economic growth, factors that together can explain why some countries have high average GDP growth and others have low average GDP growth. The terms – dependent and independent – are important, because they reflect the causal direction. GDP growth depends on the type of policy, regime, and so forth, and not the other way around. If it *is* the other way around – i.e. the policy or regime depends on GDP growth – then the explanatory framework is compromised.

The scatter diagram in Figure 1.1 illustrates the basic logic of using correlations to investigate causes of growth. The left-hand axis (the vertical or y-axis) presents the natural log of GDP per capita in current US dollars for the year 1960, based on global data, and the right-hand axis (the horizontal or x-axis) shows average GDP per capita growth rates for the period 1960–90.[11] In this example, growth is the dependent variable and income is the independent variable. The dots represent where the

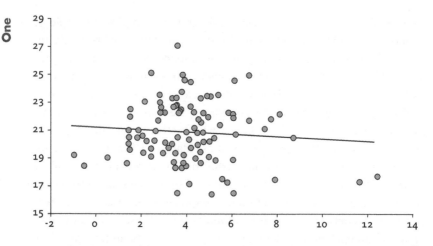

1.1 GDP in 1960 and GDP per capita growth, 1960–90 (*source*: World Bank 2014).[12]

individual countries fit with regards to GDP levels and growth rates, in what is called a scatter plot. The plot presents a snapshot of the relationship between GDP per capita in 1960 and GDP growth over the period 1960–90. The variations could be read as giving an indication of whether the total income of a country in 1960 had any effect on how quickly or slowly the country grew on average between 1960 and 1990.

There is a very weak correlation between income levels and growth; the tendency is that, on average, countries that were poorer in 1960 grew ever so slightly faster than those that were richer in 1960. This is indicated by the linear trend line that is drawn across the scatter diagram with a slight decline. If the trend line had sloped upward, it would have meant the opposite: that, on average, the poorer countries were growing more slowly than the richer ones.

This pattern matches some economic theory: for example, the advantage of relative backwardness, which is based on the assumption that it is easier and faster to adapt what leading countries have done – such as making textiles with a steam engine – than to reinvent the steam engine on your own (Gerschenkron 1962).

A scholar who is interested in whether the catch-up theory of growth is valid (see Abramovitz 1986) could then try to 'control' for other factors that might explain why some low-income countries did not grow quickly. By adding a variable to the regression that captures civil war, one might find a stronger relationship between growth and low initial income because low-income countries that experienced civil war had slow growth, and thus the investigation could reaffirm a belief in the catch-up growth hypothesis. In turn, this could lead to further research into how the fragility of states contributes to lower economic growth, and so on. This is how the cross-country growth regression literature went about it.

When Barro put his model together, the dependent variable was average growth in GDP per capita. He checked whether there were correlations between growth in GDP and other factors. He used data to measure human capital (measured as secondary and primary school enrollment), initial GDP in 1960 (to test the catch-up hypothesis) and political stability (measured by the number of revolutions and the number of assassinations).

When Barro had checked and controlled for a lot of different variables, one central finding remained. There was a large and significant African continent 'dummy variable'. A dummy variable takes the value 1 or 0; in this case it took the value 1 if the country was situated on the African continent, and 0 if it was not. In the regressions, the dummy variable remained significant. Barro's interpretation of the dummy was that the analysis had not yet fully captured the characteristics of a 'typical' African country (Barro 1991: 437).[13]

This finding prompted a research agenda that aimed to eliminate the African dummy and thereby explain the shortfall in economic growth in Africa. I have labeled the literature that shares this motivation the 'quest for the African dummy' (Jerven 2011c; see also Englebert 2000b). As we will see, the quest was ultimately unsuccessful but hugely influential.

In a review of the empirical growth literature, Durlauf and colleagues referred to this scholarly production over the following decade as a 'growth regression industry' (Durlauf et al. 2005: 599). As early as 1998, Pritchett observed that the growth experience of most developing countries had been characterized by instability rather than stable growth and warned that the 'exploding economic growth literature' was 'unlikely to be useful' (Pritchett 1998). The general growth regression literature has been described as disappointing; one assessment concluded that the 'current state of the understanding about causes of economic growth is fairly poor' and that 'we are in a weak position to explain why some countries have experienced economic growth and others not' (Kenny and Williams 2001: 15).

Yet this literature and the principal scholars who produced it have had a massive impact. Cross-country growth regressions offer an opportunity to organize statistical material, produce testable propositions, and thus advance comparisons of growth experiences, and perhaps most importantly, they allow speculation as to why some countries are poor and others rich. Precisely because of those qualities, the literature has had a major impact in academia and on policy makers and public opinion. The findings have been effectively communicated not only through journal articles but also through bestsellers written by Paul Collier, William Easterly and Jeffrey Sachs, some of the central contributors to this literature (Collier 2007; Easterly 2001c; 2006; Sachs 2005), and through the recent publication by Ndulu and colleagues of *The Political Economy of Economic Growth in Africa, 1960–2000* (Ndulu et al. 2008a; 2008b). That publication sums up the by-now widely accepted account of postcolonial economic performance in Africa, and the conclusions of Ndulu and colleagues correspond to the policy agenda set by the Bretton Woods institutions.[14]

Some of the limitations of the literature have been acknowledged. Collier and Gunning pointed out that 'one limitation of the growth regression literature is that to date it has focused upon explaining long-term average African slow growth' (Collier and Gunning 1999a: 79). Imagine you were interested in someone's history of losing and gaining body weight. If you calculated the average of monthly losses and gains over 30 years, you might find that the person gained an average of 1 ounce a month. And you could look for personal traits that explained this weight gain. If, on the other hand, you looked at the gains and losses over time, you might find that the person maintained their body weight from year 1 to year 15, then gained a lot of weight from year 16 to year 20, then maintained a steady weight from years 21 to 25, before losing weight in years 26 to 30. The second narrative is not limited by an average perspective. It might come up with a very different explanation that takes into account life changes rather than average characteristics.

Another academic, Jonathan Temple, carefully noted that 'it should perhaps go without saying that although cross-section econometrics can make a useful contribution, it can only take us so far in understanding the African experience' (Temple 1998: 343). However, interpretations of the results have often been less modest in their claims, and this literature has been *the* deliverer of the explanation for African economic performance in postcolonial Africa. For this reason, the messages of such interpretations need to be reviewed critically.

Misrepresenting the African economic growth record

The debates on African growth have been shaped by the dominant methodology used. In turn, this has determined what kind of evidence has been used and how this evidence was configured. The parameters for the discussion were set by the hypotheses that an 'African dummy' variable existed, but what was not recognized was that finding such a dummy in the first place is the result of a very specific use of the growth evidence. The African dummy derives from observing a difference between the *average* growth rates in the world as a whole and in Africa.

When I wrote my own master's thesis at the London School of Economics in 2003–04, I was struck by the focus thus far on explaining only lack of growth, but I thought it was just a legacy of the 1990s. I was surprised to find that in 2007, three years later, major publications such as *Bottom Billion* still stuck with the old line – there is no growth to explain here. Indeed, when I concluded my PhD thesis in the summer of 2008, the final sentence I wrote was:

> If it is accepted that growth revived in Africa in the early 1990s, then viewing a decade of decline as representative for African growth characteristics looks untenable, and the history of African economic growth needs to be reconsidered (Jerven 2008: 237).[15]

If that was true then, it is even truer now.

What I am presenting here is not a complete – or the only – picture of growth in African economies, I am merely suggesting that the 'chronic failure' approach is misleading. Africa's 'average growth shortfall' is what is often called a 'stylized fact'. The following figures and tables present competing shorthand ways of summarizing the postcolonial growth performance of Africa. However, the growth regression literature that relied on the stylized fact that Africa's average growth rate lagged behind that of the rest of the world since independence has had a decisive impact on the writing of the economic history of independent Africa. There are many possible ways of presenting the economic growth record of the postcolonial period. Some of them will be explored here. Of course, it is not appropriate to treat Africa as if it were a collection of homogeneous experiences. An obvious weakness of the continent-wide data is that they mask country-level performance and focus on explaining the average outcome. Moreover, it is not certain that the growth data are good enough to warrant such econometric testing (Jerven 2013b).

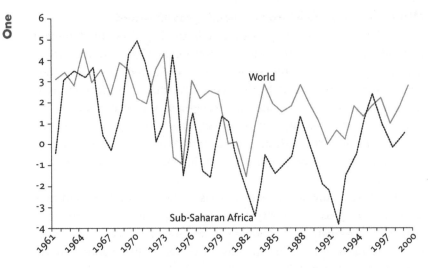

1.2 Average annual GDP growth (percentage) in sub-Saharan Africa and in the rest of the world, 1960–2000 (in constant 2000 US$) (*source*: World Bank 2007).

But we will explore those caveats later. For now, let us continue to look critically at the question *as if* it makes sense to explore the 'African' growth story as a homogeneous experience and as if the data convey a meaningful picture. The central argument pursued here, which is supported by both the aggregate evidence and country studies, is that a large number of countries experienced sustained growth before 1974, in terms of both total African GDP and country-level growth episodes, and that very few economies experienced growth in the latter half of the period (see, for example, Arrighi 2002).

Figures 1.2 and 1.3 illustrate ways of comparing growth in sub-Saharan Africa with growth in the rest of the world for the period from 1960 to 2000. Figure 1.2 plots annual growth in GDP per capita in Africa and in the rest of the world.[16] It is evident that there is a large year-to-year variation in growth and that the variation is around a higher average trend in the first half of the period than in the second half. It is also apparent that the African GDP per capita growth is often negative from the late 1970s onward. In contrast, Figure 1.3 shows the average growth in GDP per capita over the period as a conceptual approximation of the growth evidence that has informed the cross-country growth regression literature. In the regression, the average growth rate is given for each country, whereas here I have used the continent-wide average. Africa's average growth shortfall over the period is about 1.5

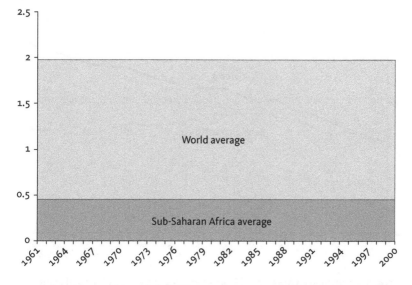

1.3 Average annual growth in GDP per capita (percentage) in sub-Saharan Africa and in the rest of the world, 1960–2000 (in constant 2000 US$) (*source*: World Bank 2007).

percent: the average African growth rate is 0.5 percent, compared with a 2 percent average for the rest of the world. This is just a comparison of average growth rates in the world and in Africa over three or four decades. Barro's cross-country regression, which used a global sample of average growth rates for the period 1960–85, found that the value for the African dummy was 1.1 percent (Barro 1991). After he included most of what he thought were the relevant factors that could explain economic growth, this average shortfall of growth between Africa and the rest of the world remained; 'solving' this growth puzzle provided the impetus for the literature on growth regression.

Finally, Figure 1.4 plots indices of GDP per capita (1960 = 1) for Africa and the rest of the world for the period 1960–2000. The main lesson to take from the indices is that the gap between the two is very small in the first part of the period; it is only after 1975 that the difference between them is larger than 10 percent. After that, however, the indices diverge dramatically. If one adopts a perspective that is not limited by a focus on the shortfall in growth average over the whole time period, the aggregate growth evidence allows for other interpretations regarding the timing of the difference. When did the negative residual accumulate? This question also shifts the focus away from

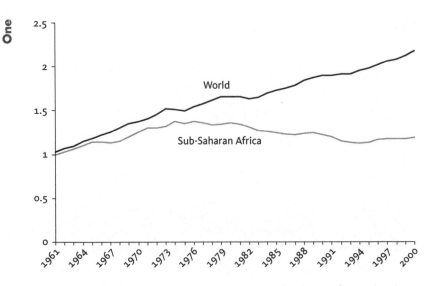

1.4 Index of annual growth in GDP per capita in sub-Saharan Africa and in the rest of the world, 1960–2000 (in constant 2000 US$; 1960 = 1) (*source*: World Bank 2007).

the reasons for a gap in growth in Africa compared with the rest of the world and toward explanations for African growth. If one judges that the growth pattern, seen in a dynamic way, does not correspond to the static approximation that relies on averages, then the regression model is unsatisfactory. This would be the case where the imagined event – a persistent negative growth residual – fails to match the real event to such an extent that it calls for different explanatory variables.

The simple point I am making is that, in contrast to what the growth literature tells us, the African growth experience has not been one of persistent stagnation. According to GDP data in international prices from the Angus Maddison dataset, the African GDP per capita in 1960 was about one-sixth of world GDP per capita.[17] This remained true until 1977, after which the gap widened, and by 2000 the African GDP per capita was less than one-tenth of world GDP per capita. The African growth shortfall is thus a more recent phenomenon: before 1977, African economies were not lagging behind significantly in terms of growth rates. Indeed, viewed in total GDP terms, the African economies grew more rapidly than those of the rest of the world in the first half of the postcolonial period, since the population growth in Africa between 1961 and 2000 was 1 percent higher than that of the rest of the world.[18] Tables 1.1 and 1.2 compare the relative performances of Africa and other regions, using total GDP indices for 1960–75 and 1975–90 respectively.

TABLE 1.1 Total GDP indices by region, 1960–75

1960 = 100	World	South Asia	East Asia	OECD	Latin America	Africa
1965	130	122	117	131	127	130
1970	171	150	164	170	168	166
1975	204	170	224	200	228	208

TABLE 1.2 Total GDP indices by region, 1975–90

1975 = 100	World	South Asia	East Asia	OECD	Latin America	Africa
1980	121	119	138	119	130	114
1985	137	156	195	135	133	120
1990	164	209	268	160	146	136

These GDP indices confirm that, for the first 15 years after independence, there was no African growth shortfall that needs to be explained. In terms of economic growth, from 1960 to 1975, African economies tended to perform better than the world average, the Organisation for Economic Co-operation and Development (OECD) economies and the South Asian economies, while they almost kept pace with the East Asian and Latin American economies. It is only in the latter period, from 1975 to 1990, that the African economies start lagging behind. In other words, before 1975 and after 1990, there is no African dummy variable that needs to be eliminated in the system of equations.

Between independence and the first oil price shock, many African countries experienced widespread economic growth. This growth was caused in part by direct and indirect state intervention; this focused on achieving industrial growth and was accompanied by growth in the agricultural sector (Jerven 2014a). Demand and prices for most African export crops were buoyant in this period as markets across the world expanded. The increase in development expenditure was financed partly by a transfer of surplus from the agriculture or mining sectors and was supported by some reliance on foreign investment and financial aid. The relative importance of these sources of funds for industrialization varied from country to country.

In 1974, the prices of food and petroleum imports soared. In addition, beginning in 1979, export prices for most agricultural crops fell and access to credit in international financial markets was temporarily scarce and expensive. The Bretton Woods institutions made financing to bridge the increasing balance-of-payment problems conditional on policy reform, and structural adjustment programs were implemented in most African countries. There is much controversy about the relative theoretical merits of both the policies that constituted the Washington Consensus package and the previous paradigm of relying on state-led development (Stein 2008).

There are some inescapable conclusions that can be reached about the implementation of structural adjustment. The reform process was lengthy and drawn out. In many countries, prolonged negotiation about structural adjustment programs delayed their implementation, not the best conceivable outcome (van de Walle 2001). But even a swift adjustment, as envisaged by the IMF and the World Bank, did not result in sustained economic growth. This has been acknowledged by both the IMF and the World Bank. The emphasis went from getting the prices right – or a liberalization of economic policy – to the importance of 'institutions' and reforms that related to 'good governance'.

The notion of African growth failure came about in the wake of the 1973–74 and 1979–81 oil price shocks and gained currency as African economies became heavily indebted under structural adjustment and required massive amounts of food aid due to the droughts that plagued the continent in the latter part of the 1975–90 period. One would expect that growth economists would have taken this specific timing into consideration when searching for the factors that explained slow growth in Africa. But they did not. In particular, the economic policies pursued by independent African economies have suffered in the assessments of growth economists. They have equated the entire postcolonial period with economic failure and have judged African economic policies and policy makers severely.

The subtraction approach

The literal interpretation of the dummy is that African economies have a persistently slower steady-state growth rate than other economies.[19] The research agenda was summed up with these words: 'it is clear that Africa has suffered a chronic failure of economic growth. The problem for analysis is to determine its causes' (Collier and Gunning 1999b: 4). The overarching question has been *why* Africa has grown slowly instead of *how* African economies have grown. The growth literature steamed ahead, and over time it proposed many different ideas about why Africa grew slowly. This meant suggesting and testing variables that supposedly captured this negative growth rate vis-à-vis the rest of the world as scholars searched for the right explanatory variable that would remove the 'stubborn African dummy' (Temple 1998: 324). At face value, this is quite a simple task – you just need to find some variables on which African countries' scores are significantly different to those of countries in other regions. Several of these were found.

According to a review of the growth literature to date, 145 explanatory variables have been found to be statistically significant (Durlauf et al. 2005: Appendix 2) and therefore can help explain the rate of growth. Of these 145 variables, some entertain similar growth hypotheses but differ in the measures used. The authors identified 43 conceptually different theories about economic growth as being 'proven' in the literature (ibid.: 639). In what follows, I will review some of the independent variables used in the regressions, assess their conceptual soundness, and test how well they stand as causal factors of growth in Africa. I will not cover all of them here.

The question I am asking is this: did the quest for the African dummy yield any results that can provide a coherent explanation for the notion that African economies grew rapidly in the 1960s and early 1970s and then declined in the late 1970s and the 1980s? My answer is no. Many variables have been found to be positively or negatively correlated with slow growth, but none of the suggested variables actually matches a coherent narrative of cause and effect. A coherent narrative has to make sense, and for the narrative to make sense it is important that cause precedes effect.

A natural starting point is the authoritative survey of the regression literature on African growth, 'Explaining African economic performance', by Paul Collier and Jan Willem Gunning (1999a; 1999b).[20] This article grouped the most significant factors in African growth regressions into six categories: lack of social capital, lack of openness to trade, deficient public services, geography and risk, lack of financial depth, and high aid dependency.

I call this method of investigation a 'subtraction approach', where the characteristics of a developed country are compared with the characteristics of an underdeveloped country. The differences between them are taken to explain slow growth. The list of factors above fits this pattern:

the lack of growth is explained by the lack of something else. Linked with the subtraction approach is the revival of the notion of the vicious circle of underdevelopment, where underdevelopment explains itself. It so happens that a ranking of countries according to their average rate of economic growth from 1960 to 1990 is very similar to a ranking by absolute income levels in 2000. As a result, the task of explaining slow recent economic growth has been confused with that of explaining the long-term condition of underdevelopment.

Observing the difference between two countries based on a subtraction approach is potentially a useful start, but it yields a useless conclusion. One has to ask why a difference exists and how it came about. The basic fact that correlation does not imply causation needs to be restated forcefully when assessing the regression work on African growth. Correlation and circular reasoning do not make us wiser; what is needed is a stricter explanatory framework of cause and effect. The independent variables suggested in the literature may fit with the stylized fact of persistent stagnation, but they do not explain a change in economic performance.

The problem with the focus on slow growth is that it is not compatible with the actual growth record. As we just saw, African economies have displayed both growth and decline; they have not been trapped in a low-level equilibrium where poverty has reproduced itself. As a result, the factors suggested in the subtraction approach and the circular reasoning in which they are embedded are not convincing and do not provide useful insight. We know that Africa has performed relatively worse than the rest of the world in terms of average GDP per capita growth over the postcolonial period as a whole. We also know that, on average, African economies are poorer than the average of the economies of the rest of the world. Therefore, we can also assume that they would rank lower on indicators of education, health and infrastructure. It is also reasonable to assume that these poor countries receive more aid and have less-developed financial markets. The regression literature confirmed all this. What it did not do was explain how African economies could grow and then decline.

Not only was the analytical framework for conducting comparisons flawed, but the variables that were supposed to capture differences in policies and institutions had a very specific shortcoming. Either their average values were inflated by the economic shocks of the late 1970s and early 1980s or the observations were made in the 1980s, after the economic shocks had already occurred. It is highly misleading to use these post-shock phenomena that are essentially effects of a growth failure as causes that explain economic performance over the entire period of from 1960 to 1990. The growth literature used effects and outcomes of economic turbulence in the 1980s and the direct symptoms of these economic shocks as causal variables that explained the imagined event of persistent slow growth. Collier and Gunning summarized a decade of research into the causes of economic growth as follows: countries that grew slower on average between 1960 and 1990 had poorer education, received more aid and had worse financial and physical infrastructures. That is a fair descriptive statement, but the growth literature made a very specific causal argument. It argued that these variables were evidence of 'bad' policies and that it was these growth-inhibiting policies that caused slow growth.

Aid dependency

Collier and Gunning illustrated the shortcomings of using effect to explain cause very clearly when arguing that Africa suffers from high aid dependency and that this has caused slow growth. To make their case they reported that, in 1994, the ratio of aid to gross national product (GNP) in Africa was almost five times higher than in other low-income countries (Collier and Gunning 1999a: 74). That is an impressive statistic. But it makes you wonder how it compares across time and space and why they chose 1994. The World Development Indicators (WDI) record aid

1.5 Financial aid as a percentage of GNI for sub-Saharan Africa, 1960–2000 (*source*: World Bank 2002).

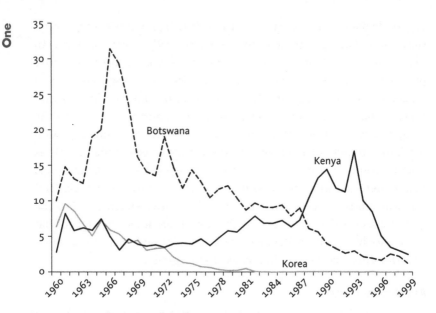

1.6 Financial aid as a percentage of GNI for Korea, Kenya and Botswana, 1960–99 (*source*: World Bank 2012).

dependency ratios as a percentage of gross national income (GNI), which includes official development assistance, official aid, technical cooperation, and all loans with at least a 25 percent grant element (World Bank 2002). The percentages for sub-Saharan Africa are plotted in Figure 1.5.

Figure 1.5 reveals that when Collier and Gunning chose the year 1994, they chose the absolute peak observation. Relatively high aid dependency is indeed a symptom of the growth experience of the 1980s. However, the extreme values of this statistic are a recent phenomenon and a result of the growth failure and the ensuing structural adjustment lending from 1979 onward; they cannot be accepted as a causal factor that explains growth performance since 1960. For an illustrative example, compare the data for Kenya, Botswana and Korea presented in Figure 1.6. Korea received more aid than Kenya in the early period, and the spike in official development assistance in Kenya in the 1990s is directly caused by the donor aid and loans that were disbursed in this decade in order to finance structural adjustment programs.

While there have been vivid debates about whether or not development aid contributes to growth, the argument that high aid dependency is a direct cause of slow growth does not make empirical sense. The claim is made based on correlations of averages of 'aid' and 'growth', but the static average does not match up with the history of economic growth in Africa. The most elaborate attempt to make this argument work was carried out by Craig Burnside and David Dollar (2000). In their version of the regressions, it turns out that aid works,[21] but only if it coincides with 'good' policies.

That sounds very similar to saying that 'aid works when it works, except when it doesn't'. Good policies are hard to define and even harder to measure precisely. To capture 'bad' policies, Burnside and Dollar used variables such as high inflation, high premiums for currency in black markets, and budget deficits. But these are not measures of economic policies per se; these variables are economic outcomes of a decline in economic growth. High inflation, high deficits and foreign exchange shortages are all symptoms of economic distress or external shocks – and, just like high aid dependency, they are better considered as results of a decline in economic growth, not as causes of that decline. A cause should precede an effect. If things happen the other way around, causality is reversed.

Deficient public services

In terms of human development, Africa has not been a chronic failure in the postcolonial period. Significant progress has been made in health and education since independence (Sender 1999). Services have been expanded, even during times of constrained finances and external demands for austerity. Thus, the term 'deficient public services' does not capture the trend or change in public service delivery in African economies. Bennell (2002: 1186) argues that Africa has been extraordinary in this respect and reminds us that, in Europe and North America, the expansion of education coincided with a rapid growth of the formal sector, while African countries have promoted formal education without there being a demand for educated laborers and in the midst of economic crisis and contraction.

Even so, the growth regression literature has zeroed in on the relationship between growth and human capital. Collier and Gunning (1999a: 71) noted that 'the public service which has received most attention in growth regressions has been education', although they conceded that issues relating to education and its link to growth 'are unresolved'. Enrollment in education and literacy levels have increased rapidly even when the growth rate has not been high (Pritchett 2001). Actually, if you plot growth and literacy rates from 1970 to 2000 using

World Bank data, you find an almost perfect negative correlation.[22] If you believed that correlation is causation, this would imply that increased literacy has a negative impact on growth rates. That is not the case. The observed pattern reflects the fact that there has been an impressive improvement in human capital in African economies since independence and that this trend has continued despite the slowdown in growth since the mid-1970s.

So can you still argue that education has a negative effect on growth? Yes. This contradictory evidence can be accommodated in a growth regression. If one were to regress a relative deficit in human capital in Africa compared with the rest of the world, the result would be that human capital development would have a significant negative effect on growth. According to this method, human capital would be found to account for 1.2 percent of Africa's annual growth shortfall relative to Asia.[23] But in that case, did a researcher simply obtain a statistically significant result, or was something actually explained?

In theory, it can be argued that there is a certain threshold of human capital beyond which African economies would start to benefit from growth based on human capital. This remains an untested, unstated and (importantly) unproven hypothesis. In the growth literature it was argued that a lack of education had been the chief constraint on growth in Africa.[24] Education may be seen more correctly as an end in itself, and then the question should not be whether there is a static education shortfall with respect to other countries, but rather how African governments are doing in terms of delivering education.

Bad policies

The central argument in the growth literature fitted very well with a 1981 World Bank report (called the Berg report) that provided the rationale for structural adjustment (World Bank 1981). The report called for liberal reforms such as devaluing exchange rates, increasing the prices of agricultural crops, reducing subsidies for urban consumers, downsizing state bureaucracies, and privatizing state-owned enterprises. This matches the list of policy mistakes, or growth-inhibiting policies, that the growth regression literature has identified. However, when the reforms were implemented in the 1980s and 1990s, growth did not return (Easterly 2001c). Instead, decline deepened, and because governments based their political stability on systems of rents and patronage, many faced a serious crisis of legitimacy (Jerven 2010b).

It could be seen as a real paradox that the growth literature gives policy such a prominent role in explanations for slow growth, because most African economies grew rapidly precisely when 'bad' policies were initially implemented (Collier and Gunning 1999a). The first structural adjustment package was agreed upon with Senegal in 1979 (van de Walle 2001). Since then, although most African economies have been implementing or moving toward the 'good' policies prescribed by orthodox economists, economic performance has been poor. Although there is considerable debate about whether these policies have been implemented fully, the reforms that were put in place specifically targeted the prominent variables in the regression literature. There was a general move toward liberalization. Price controls, restrictions on international trade and fixed exchange rates were abandoned. There were privatizations and financial reforms and there was a general decrease in state intervention and expenditure.

A classic example of trying to capture the effect of excessive state intervention is the use of the black market premium variable. The dataset for this variable has been compiled from observations of black market exchange rates in currency yearbooks.[25] In theory, the black market premium could be a measure of distortions caused by governments' interventions in markets: that is to say, governments attempt to fix the prices of foreign exchange and the black market rates capture the gap between the official price and the market price. In the 1960s and the 1970s, most countries in the world were on a fixed exchange rate system, and although some African currencies were systematically overvalued (this does not apply to the francophone countries), the extreme values that inflated the measure were outcomes of economic shocks, not government policies (Azam 2007). The time aspect of the black market premium in the underlying dataset confirms this. The years with very high values in the late 1970s and early 1980s coincide with external economic shocks, and the highest observed black market rates followed directly from the currency devaluations imposed by structural adjustment. In addition, the observations of 'industrial countries' in the dataset are not real data. Instead, the values for industrial countries are added as zero. In other words, according to this metric, there are by definition no government interventions that distort markets in developed countries (Easterly 2001b). Moreover, as the data bear out, there is nothing particularly 'African' about having black market premiums. Figure 1.7 shows that Senegal had consistently

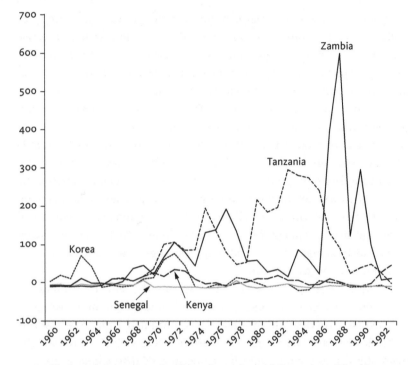

1.7 Black market premiums for Kenya, Korea, Senegal, Tanzania and Zambia, 1960–93 (percentages) (*source*: Easterly 2001c).

low black market premiums and that the black market rates in Korea were higher than in three African economies in the 1960s and higher than those in both Kenya and Senegal in the 1970s.

In fact, Easterly and colleagues carefully noted that black market premiums were a bad proxy for policy: 'If shock variables are omitted, estimates of the effect of the black market premium on growth will falsely attribute externally-induced adversity to policy' (Easterly et al. 1993: 474). Yet this warning was not heeded. The pattern from the other growth determinants is repeated – post-shock factors are falsely used to account for both policies and growth for the whole period.

The 'bad' policies that have been identified in the literature can also be seen as outcomes of the economic shocks. As resources grew short following the shocks, institutional quality deteriorated. Inflation decreased the real value of public servants' salaries, providing incentives for corruption. The time horizon shortened for political leaders and the incentives, as well as the opportunities, for destructive rent-seeking behavior increased. Black market premiums were an indication of a shortage of foreign currency and of the fact that policy makers restricted access to imports and foreign currency in response to a balance-of-payment crisis. Meanwhile, development expenditures and public service delivery were compromised by a lack of revenue. As a result of all these things, many of the impressive gains countries had made since independence were reversed.

While it is true that state interventions in most African economies have left a lot to be desired in terms of achieving economic development outcomes, this should neither be taken to mean that African governments have consistently chosen 'growth-inhibiting policies' nor explained as an inevitable outcome of 'African' conditions. A methodologically sound historical account avoids using the effect to explain the cause. In the economic history of postcolonial Africa, this has proved to be particularly challenging, as the effect – the African growth failure – has loomed large. The prevailing development policy paradigm has given impetus to a typology of 'good' policies versus 'bad' policies. 'Bad' policies are hard to define precisely, and it is not enough to identify them as less-than-perfect decisions. To expect African policy makers in the 1960s and 1970s to have had foresight regarding economic change and to have transcended contemporary policy advice seems to be asking too much of them. The fact that information is less than perfect is common to both state and market decisions. That decisions are constrained by the information available to the decision makers is one of the central limitations that make economic policies less than ideal. It is fair to point out this deficiency, but more caution should be exercised in practical and relative comparisons of the economic development experience. Instead, the growth literature went one step further and assigned specific blame for the 'bad policies' – the problem of African economies was 'bad governance'.

Bad governance

I have shown that there is more than reasonable doubt concerning the direct causal link between the typologies of 'good' and 'bad' economic policies and the economic growth record. In the early growth literature, it was enough to show correlation between 'bad' policies and slow economic growth to suggest that such policies were also the cause of that slow growth. However, slow growth and policy outcomes such as high inflation are, of course, both outcomes. This amounts to a serious problem of reversal causality, or what economists call the 'endogeneity' problem. This problem was accepted as an inherent deficiency in the analysis of concurrent economic events at first, but this changed over time and it was increasingly felt that it was not slow growth that needed to be explained; instead, the research problem became the identification of the kinds of political and social arrangements and systems that consistently produced 'bad' policies. Such arrangements and systems were summarized as 'bad governance', or as institutions that were the result of damaging initial conditions or unfortunate historical legacies. This shift in focus created the basis for what I call the second generation of growth literature.

The regression literature increasingly blamed African policy makers for poor economic performance. The research strategy of relating policy to growth was sidestepped. Instead, researchers traced 'the choice of bad policies ... to the lack of social capital and deficient political institutions' (Azam et al. 2002: 177). Jonathan Temple summed up the consensus in the literature when he stated that 'observable variables capturing initial conditions can account for around three-quarters of the variation in developing country growth rates. These variables affect growth mainly by determining policy outcomes' (Temple 1998: 341). The regression literature initially found that it was better to consider certain policy variables as outcomes. These variables, which included overvalued currencies, corruption and general institutional quality, were correlated with low average growth rates. But if that was the case, then why did certain countries elect bad leaders and others elect good leaders?

The growth literature wanted to explain 'bad' policies by pointing to social arrangements that were specific to Africa. The term that was later used to describe these arrangements was 'institutions', but Collier and Gunning referred to them as 'lack of social capital' and suggested that this could explain why Africa performed so poorly. The argument Collier and Gunning made in their synthesis of the regression literature was that a lack of social capital is Africa's 'original sin' from which all growth-retarding factors can be derived. According to their view, a low level of 'social capital' has 'large, damaging effects on the growth rate' (Collier and Gunning 1999a: 74). It causes 'bad' policies such as restrictive trade policies and deficient public services, intensifies the effect of unfavorable natural endowments, has a lack of financial depth as a by-product, and makes aid inefficient.

The challenge was to find social, political or even cultural variables that were considered to be 'exogenous' to the economic process but that one could still plausibly use to assign some sort of causal link. As early as the late 1990s, the list of what was fundamentally wrong with African societies had grown quite long, and it was on the basis of research to that date that *The Economist* asked in 2000: does Africa have a character flaw? The answer, according to some economists, was yes: corruption is endemic, bureaucracy is inefficient, contracts cannot be enforced, countries are ravaged by civil war, and this is all due to a combination of inequality, ethnic fragmentation and low social development, depending on which economist you asked. A sample menu is provided in Table 1.3.

TABLE 1.3 Evidence used in the empirical growth literature for 'lack of social capital'

	Sub-Saharan Africa	Other less-developed countries (LDCs)
Corruption[1]	4.97	6.03
Bureaucracy[2]	1.38	1.72
Enforceability of contracts[3]	1.95	2.09
Civil war (months per year)	1.27	0.72
Fractionalization[4]	67.6	32.7
Social development[5]	1.10	-0.43
Inequality[6]	31.0	31.0

Notes: 1. Data from the *International Country Risk Guide* for 1982; a low score indicates a high level of corruption. 2. Data from the *International Country Risk Guide* for 1982; high scores indicate better quality, with the range 0–6. 3. Data from the Business Environmental Risk Intelligence dataset for 1972; low scores indicate weak enforceability, with the range 0–4. 4. The range is 0–100, with completely homogeneous societies scored as zero. 5. The Adelman-Morris Index of 'social development' as of the early 1960s was constructed with an effective range of 1.86 (for the least developed) to -1.91 (the most developed) for 74 countries that Adelman and Morris classified as developing at the time. 6. The income share of the third and fourth quintiles.

Sources: Corruption and fractionalization from Mauro (1995); civil war (months per year) from Singer and Small (1994); Adelman-Morris Index and inequality from Temple (1998). This table is reproduced from Collier and Gunning (1999a: 67, Table 2: Socio-political indicators: differences between sub-Saharan Africa and other LDCs).

First, note that all the measures of institutional quality are observations from the latter half of the period analyzed. Consequently, these are likely to be the effects of the growth failure of the early 1980s and not a cause of the growth rate during the whole period from 1960 to

2000. The data are also far from comprehensive. In a landmark study of institutional quality, Daniel Kaufmann used only two African countries, South Africa and Nigeria (Kaufmann et al. 1999). These authors use the same source for data on corruption and bureaucratic inefficiency as Paolo Mauro used, and this contains data from only ten African countries, including the notorious and not necessarily representative Nigeria, Zaire and Cameroon (Mauro 1995).

By explaining the African growth failure using subjective indexes of institutional corruption and efficiency constructed in the mid-1980s, economists are essentially explaining the outcome with an effect. The data on civil war are more comprehensive, but it is important to note that one of the most supported hypothesis in the quantitative study of the causes of civil·war is that economic shocks increase the probability of the onset of war (Miguel et al. 2004; Blattman and Miguel 2010). Thus, there is no clear evidence to show whether the causality runs from growth to civil war or the other way round.

The two variables of interest in Table 1.7 are ethnicity and social development, as these opened up a new line of inquiry. Their key advantage was that they were taken from the 1950s and 1960s, so they could not be effects of economic growth from the 1960s onward. As early as 1981, Robert Bates offered a seminal explanation based in rational choice theory for why growth-retarding policies were adopted in the first place, arguing that African politicians chose policies that served their own interests rather than those that favored economic development (Bates 1981).[26]

As we will see, what I call the second generation of growth literature ventured further down this path by suggesting that a lack of growth and lack of pro-growth policies could be explained by 'initial conditions', using measures for the lack of state legitimacy, lack of social capital and ethnic diversity to explain why African states were incapable of development (Englebert 2000a; Temple 1998; Easterly and Levine 1997). We will explore this literature in the next chapter. But the idea that initial conditions in Africa directly determined persistent slow growth does not make sense. There was growth in the 1960s and 1970s and again in the late 1990s. At best, variables that are supposed to capture initial conditions can be seen as contingent upon other factors: for example, 'political representation of certain ethnic groups was not considered a problem until coffee prices fell', or 'when rainfall failure made land scarcity more pressing'. Such a diagnosis would have lent credence to a story that emphasized external shocks and downplayed policy and governance, but it was rejected. Based on the evidence, it seems that unfortunate initial conditions were overcome in Africa, and how or whether they came into play at a later stage could be part of a historical explanation – but the regression literature had no room for such an explanation.

A leap of faith

The explanation offered by cross-sectional growth regression for slow growth in postcolonial Africa is incoherent. The fundamental problem is that it does not match the record of growth. A static representation of the African growth shortfall has become dominant and it has been tempting to interpret the dummy variable as a 'character flaw' in Africa that has made the continent incapable of economic development. However, the growth record tells a different story. An account of growth in Africa that takes the qualitative and quantitative changes into consideration, explaining African growth as it happened and not as an averaged negative residual, might reach very different conclusions from the ones on offer in the regression literature.

It requires a leap of faith to go from cross-sectional observations to the verdict that such observations are valid over time and across localities. Before taking such a leap, it is worth reminding ourselves of two things. First, the failure to fully recognize the importance of external factors misled supporters of structural adjustment to expect a swift return to growth in African economies. Second, the failure to recognize the specific constraints and characteristics of individual economies and African regions meant that reforms were poorly designed and implemented. By not taking temporal and spatial specifics into account, the African growth literature continues to draw a misleading veil over Africa's growth processes. The growth of the 1960s and 1970s was missed, as was the recent return to economic growth at the end of the 1990s.

Important quantitative and qualitative changes took place in Africa over the period from 1960 to 2000. The pattern consisted of growth followed by decline, not a permanent stagnation. This observation raises the issue of timing and missed events in the performance narrative. The growth literature skirted across two decades of structural adjustment and falsely attributed observations from the 1980s to the whole period while ignoring the simultaneous policy changes. The focus on average growth also meant that some of the factors that were problematic for the mainstream policy explanation were circumvented.

To disentangle this muddle of initial conditions, income levels, growth rates and causes and effects, it is necessary to bring time and change into the equation. Time and change are often taken to mean history, so this may sound like saying that history matters. However, as history became part of the toolbox of the growth economists, it took a very specific form. Instead of investigating the historical pattern of growth in Africa, the new literature took its impetus from the growth literature and took it as a given that failure was chronic, and thus the task was to find out why Africa was trapped in history.

2 | Trapped in history?

'Avanti, economic historians!' sounded the call from Patrick Manning to African economic historians in 1987 (Manning 1987). But instead of forging ahead, the discipline arguably went into decline. The history of economic development in Africa became almost exclusively an exercise for development economists, while historians focused on other topics. Until recently, most economists working on Africa took 1960 as their starting point. However, during the past ten years there has been a surge in quantitative research on African development. In particular, attempts have been made to establish relationships between historical events and current income levels and inequalities.

The search for the historical roots of poverty has created a renewed interest in African economic history (Hopkins 2009). Economists, having agreed some time ago that institutions matter (see, for example, Bardhan 2005), now seem to be forming a new consensus around another truism. This time, it is history that matters (Nunn 2009; Woolcock et al. 2009; Guinnane et al. 2004).

If one accepts the stylized fact of persistent growth failure in post-colonial Africa and approaches economic growth as a linear concept, the next logical step is – and indeed has been – a search for the root cause of underdevelopment.[1] The assumption is that low income today must be the result of lack of growth in the past. The first generation of empirical growth literature explained the lack of growth in postcolonial Africa by linking slow growth to measures of low institutional quality and proxies for growth-retarding policies (Collier and Gunning 1999a; Jerven 2011c). Metrics that were meant to capture a lack of openness to trade, state intervention in markets and other variables were found to correlate with, and were argued to be causally related to, slow growth in Africa. But increasingly these were also considered to be just that – correlated outcomes. Consequently, they needed to be explained by an underlying cause, or at least something had to be changed in order to verify the direction of causation. This is where history came in so handy.

A noted complaint from economic historians about economists' work on African development was that 1960 was conventionally taken as a starting point, as if the period before this point, and therefore African economic history, had no relevance for economic policy today (Hopkins 1986; Manning 1987; Austin 2007). There has been a definite change of emphasis in recent years as economists have begun to take both the precolonial and colonial histories of Africa into consideration. The seminal contribution here was made by Acemoglu, Johnson and Robinson, who argued that different patterns of colonization have had a persistent impact on economic growth through 'institutions' (Acemoglu et al. 2002). Douglass North (1990) defined institutions as 'the rules of the game', or humanly devised rules that constrain behavior. In a nutshell, the argument is that some places are richer because they have institutions that are good for growth – such as patent laws – whereas other areas are poorer because they have institutions that are bad for growth – such as norms or laws that inhibit innovation or equal gender participation in the labor market. The suggestion was that these different institutional settings had a historical cause, and the growth equations in the second generation of the literature began to span several centuries. But, paradoxically, when the economists explained very long-term growth, they did so using only evidence from a very recent past.

The historical evidence of growth

Economic historians welcomed explorations of the historical roots of economic conditions, albeit with some reservations. Austin called contributions such as the thesis suggested by Acemoglu, Johnson and Robinson a 'compression of history' (Austin 2008b). Why was history compressed? In essence, the problem is that no African GDP datasets with growth time series go back further than 1950. Studies of economic growth have thus been confined to the postcolonial period, simply because there are no datasets available for earlier periods. One example of missing data is provided by Artadi and Sala-i-Martin, who wrote an article called 'The economic tragedy of the XX century'. Based on their title, one might reasonably expect to see some evidence from the earlier part of the century in their study, but the data Artadi and Sala-i-Martin marshaled cover only the period from 1960 to 2002 (Artadi and Sala-i-Martin 2003). Only about 40 percent of the century is included, and the remaining 60 years are just assumed to have had no importance.

Of course, there is information and evidence about long-term economic history, and there are even GDP data that go further back in time.

The most widely used resource and the one that currently provides the longest time series is the Maddison dataset (Maddison 2009).

TABLE 2.1 African and world GDP per capita, 1–1950 CE

	1	1000	1500	1600	1700	1820	1870	1900	1913	1940	1950
Total Africa	472	425	414	422	421	420	500	601	637	813	889
World	467	453	566	596	615	667	871	1,262	1,525	1,958	2,109

Notes: All values are in constant 1990 international Geary–Khamis dollars. The only African countries for which Maddison has individual income estimates for this period are Algeria, Egypt, Libya, Tunisia and Morocco.

Source: Maddison 2009.

This dataset includes annual international GDP per capita data for all African countries for the period from 1950 to 2006, although it incorporates observations for the continent as a whole back to year 1. There are significant problems with this dataset.

The aggregate picture that is drawn in Table 2.1 does not reflect what is known about periods of export growth, state formation and wealth accumulation in parts of Africa. According to Maddison's estimates, African GDP per capita for the years 1500, 1600, 1700 and 1820 was 414, 422, 421 and 420 respectively. There were large flows of commodities and factors of production, both internally and externally, during the Atlantic slave trade and the cash crop revolution. Kingdoms rose and fell, colonial empires were established, and railways and mines were developed, and yet the GDP per capita measure in the Maddison dataset barely blinks. The African GDP series from year 1 to 1950 is inaccurate and incredible. Moreover, it inadvertently distorts our view of history. The problem with having only one number for one continent with one observation every century or so is that it gives the impression that there is very little history to explain. It can also be taken to support the notion that Africa has always been poor and has been permanently stuck in growth failure.

Indeed, David Bloom and Jeffrey Sachs use an earlier version of the Maddison data for that purpose. They conclude that, for the past two centuries, 'Africa's poor economic growth has been chronic rather than episodic' (Bloom and Sachs 1998: 208). In Chapter 3, I will show that this paints a misleading picture of African economic history. Well-documented growth in African markets for currency, labor and goods led to Smithian growth through specialization in some areas (Hopkins 1973). Moreover, the Atlantic trade brought new technology, for instance the introduction of new cultigens that must have led to increased total factor productivity (Austin 2008a: 588; Jerven 2010b). In addition, the economic growth that occurred in Africa could not have happened without significant investment in perennial crops, land improvement and transportation infrastructure. Finally, these growth episodes led to historically documented changes such as new markets in land and labor, strengthened states, and improved living standards. Lasting and recurring economic growth episodes spurred political and institutional change. It would be a mistake to interpret the economic history of Africa as if modern economic growth had never touched the continent.

But instead of focusing on such trajectories of growth and seeking to explain them, economists took an analytical shortcut in the second generation of the growth literature. In their defense, this stance was necessitated by the paucity of evidence, but it led economists astray. The new regressions stopped using 'growth', as measured by the percentage rate of change in GDP, as evidence; instead, they switched to explaining country-level variations in 'income' as measured by GDP per capita today. When is today? For most of these regressions, 'today' was the year 2000. As already noted, in principle the link made in the economic growth literature between growth and income is fairly straightforward: low income today must be the result of a lack of income growth in the past. The next step is where it gets complicated. Because no GDP statistics go back very far in time, the growth regression literature has not provided any evidence to demonstrate that it can explain the differences in long-term growth rates; it just asks us to take the leap of faith that the distribution of GDP per capita in the year 2000 contains some cumulative difference that regressions can exploit to tease out theories about why some countries have been successful and others have not.

Of course, this approach, since it does not have any history, runs the risk of neglecting important developments that took place between time $t = 0$ and today. Growth has been episodic in African countries, and it is a major challenge to establish the correct point in time when the historical roots of growth can be judged to have manifested themselves. There is a considerable danger that the metric one chooses to describe the prosperity of a polity within geographical boundaries and at a particular time may be inaccurate and therefore not representative of the historical experience.

Explaining variation in income 'today'

How meaningful is a GDP per capita estimate today? Can it be used to establish a ranking for one country and to compare it with another? I asked myself that question when I saw the research papers of authors such as Nathan Nunn (2007; 2008). In his 2008 paper he argued that there was a correlation between numbers of slaves exported (during a very long period, and before the countries of today actually existed, but let us ignore that for a moment) and GDP today. If that exercise is to make any sense, then we must first be sure that GDP today is a meaningful measure. In a research article for *African Affairs* (Jerven 2010d), I subjected the GDP per capita evidence of African countries to three tests: one for accuracy, one for reliability, and one for volatility.

First, I carried out a simple comparison of the GDP per capita estimate in the datasets that are used most often for cross-country regressions: the Maddison dataset, the Penn World Tables and the WDI.[2]

The three sources agree on the ranking of some countries but disagree on the rankings of most. In some cases, the discrepancy is large. All three datasets agree that the Democratic Republic of Congo (DRC), formerly Zaire, is the poorest country, but any agreement stops there. Only six countries appear among the ten poorest economies in all three databases. In addition to the DRC, these are Sierra Leone, Niger, Burundi, Tanzania and Ethiopia. There is more consensus about which are the ten richest countries. Even though there is wide variation in how the three databases rank these countries, they agree about nine of the countries that appear in the top ten (see Table 2.2).

There are also large fluctuations in the rankings across the three databases. The highest degree of uncertainty concerns Guinea, which is ranked as the seventh poorest economy according to the Maddison dataset, while in the Penn World Tables it misses the category of the ten richest African countries by just one place. The WDI rank Mozambique as one of the eight poorest countries, while the Maddison dataset places it among the 12 richest economies. Across the three sources, the ranking of Liberia jumps 20 places: the Penn World Tables rank it the second poorest nation in sub-Saharan Africa, while the Maddison dataset sees it as being richer than the majority of sub-Saharan African countries. Angola, the Central African Republic, Comoros, Congo-Brazzaville, Nigeria and Zambia all make leaps of more than ten places in the rankings from one source to another, leaving the relative ranking of one-fifth of the countries a matter of great uncertainty.

TABLE 2.2 Relative income ranking in Africa from lowest to highest according to three data sources for the year 2000

	Maddison		World Development Indicators		Penn World Tables	
1	Democratic Republic of Congo	217	Democratic Republic of Congo	92	Democratic Republic of Congo	359
2	Sierra Leone	410	Ethiopia	115	Liberia	472
3	Chad	429	Burundi	139	Sierra Leone	684
4	Niger	486	Sierra Leone	153	Burundi	699
5	Burundi	496	Malawi	169	Ethiopia	725
6	Tanzania	535	Tanzania	190	Guinea-Bissau	762
7	Guinea	572	Liberia	191	Niger	807
8	Central African Republic	576	Mozambique	191	Tanzania	817
9	Comoro Islands	581	Niger	200	Togo	823
10	Ethiopia	605	Guinea-Bissau	210	Madagascar	823
11	Togo	614	Chad	218	Chad	830
12	Zambia	645	Rwanda	242	Malawi	839
13	Malawi	656	Burkina Faso	243	Zambia	866
14	Guinea-Bissau	681	Madagascar	246	Burkina Faso	933
15	Madagascar	706	Nigeria	254	Central African Republic	945
16	Angola	765	Mali	294	Gambia	954
17	Uganda	797	Sudan	313	Rwanda	1,018
18	Rwanda	819	Togo	323	Mali	1,047
19	Mali	892	Kenya	328	Sudan	1,048
20	Gambia	895	Central African Republic	339	Uganda	1,058
21	Burkina Faso	921	São Tomé and Príncipe	341	Nigeria	1,074
22	Liberia	990	Uganda	348	Mozambique	1,093

	Country	Value	Country	Value	Country	Value
23	Sudan	991	Gambia	370	Benin	1,251
24	Mauritania	1,017	Zambia	394	Kenya	1,268
25	Kenya	1,031	Ghana	413	Congo-Brazzaville	1,286
26	Cameroon	1,082	Benin	414	São Tomé and Príncipe	1,300
27	São Tomé and Príncipe	1,226	Comoros	436	Comoros	1,359
28	Nigeria	1,251	Mauritania	495	Ghana	1,392
29	Ghana	1,270	Angola	524	Mauritania	1,521
30	Benin	1,283	Lesotho	548	Senegal	1,571
31	Zimbabwe	1,328	Guinea	605	Lesotho	1,834
32	Côte d'Ivoire	1,352	Senegal	609	Angola	1,975
33	Senegal	1,358	Zimbabwe	620	Côte d'Ivoire	2,171
34	Mozambique	1,365	Cameroon	675	Cameroon	2,472
35	Lesotho	1,490	Côte d'Ivoire	739	Guinea	2,546
36	Cape Verde	1,777	Congo-Brazzaville	791	Zimbabwe	3,256
37	Congo-Brazzaville	2,005	Swaziland	1,538	Cape Verde	4,984
38	Swaziland	2,630	Cape Verde	1,541	Namibia	5,269
39	Namibia	3,637	Equatorial Guinea	1,599	Equatorial Guinea	6,495
40	Gabon	3,847	Namibia	2,366	Botswana	7,256
41	South Africa	3,978	Botswana	3,931	South Africa	8,226
42	Botswana	4,269	South Africa	4,020	Swaziland	8,517
43	Seychelles	6,354	Mauritius	4,104	Gabon	10,439
44	Equatorial Guinea	7,973	Gabon	4,378	Seychelles	10,593
45	Mauritius	10,652	Seychelles	6,557	Mauritius	15,121

Sources: Maddison 2003; Heston et al. 2006; World Bank 2007.

The average variation in the whole sample is seven places; this is calculated as the sum of the highest minus the lowest ranking for each country divided by the number of countries. If this average variation is accepted as a basis for creating cohorts of countries, the sample can be neatly divided into three groups: low-income, middle-income and high-income African economies, where the middle of each cohort is ranked as eighth, twenty-third and thirty-eighth respectively (see Table 2.3).[3] The conclusion of the accuracy test is summed up in Table 2.3. There are not 45 clearly distinguishable levels of GDP per capita for these countries; instead, they are better placed in three groups, in which there is a lot of variation in the relative ranking according to data source.

TABLE 2.3 Low-, middle- and high-income African economies for the year 2000

Low-income	Middle-income	High-income
Democratic Republic of Congo	Uganda	Zimbabwe
Niger	Sudan	Gabon
Burundi	São Tomé and Príncipe	Namibia
Sierra Leone	Mali	Côte d'Ivoire
Ethiopia	Mauritania	South Africa
Guinea-Bissau	Ghana	Equatorial Guinea
Chad	Gambia	Cape Verde
Malawi	Kenya	Botswana
Madagascar	Benin	Mauritius
Tanzania		Swaziland
		Seychelles

Sources: Heston et al. 2006; World Bank 2007.

The accuracy test left 29 countries.[4] But what about the reliability of the estimates? This is the second test I conducted. We know that some GDP per capita estimates are not really firm data points but might better be considered as a midpoint in a band of variation. In my exercise, I chose a band of variation of plus or minus 30 percent, although recent changes in GDP estimates for some countries may indicate that this is on the low side; for example, Ghana's GDP almost doubled when the country revised its national estimates in 2010 (Jerven 2013a). Table 2.4 lists the high and low estimates for the 29 countries and shows how these estimates affected the relative ranking of each country according to the system I established in Table 2.3.[5]

The average income in this sample according to the Maddison dataset is $2,145. The mean is considerably higher than the median income. Kenya is situated at the middle of the 29-country sample, with an income of $1,031. According to the implied ranking in the Maddison dataset, Kenya is either the sixth poorest country or the eighth richest country, or anywhere in between those two points. The data about the distribution of income among African economies have a much longer tail toward the higher income section: the GDP per capita of Sierra Leone is a bit less than half that of Kenya, and the per capita income in Mauritius is more than ten times higher than Kenya's. The reliability test also shows that it is hard to distinguish the 'low-income' from the 'middle-income' countries in the sample.

One well-known characteristic of African income is its volatility. This is due in part to four factors: low absolute income; the dominance of the agricultural sector on the continent, which makes income particularly dependent on variations in the weather; the continent's dependence on fluctuating world market prices; and, finally, variations in the statistical practices of national statistics bureaus, which may include abrupt ad hoc changes in income estimates. Thus, it might seem arbitrary to choose a year in which the historical legacy is supposed to have manifested itself in a low or a high income. Although, from a pragmatic point of view, it makes sense to use a point in time that is relatively close to 'today' when examining income distribution, an investigation of lasting historical legacies should be corroborated by an examination of the validity of the statistical correlation that supports the research findings through time. This does not mean that the relative ranking of income should be constant over time. However, if the relative ranking of economies is very volatile, a good case can be made that the kind of research required is an investigation into trajectories of economic growth and economic change rather than analyses that aim to explain an assumed stable distribution of income between countries.

In order to eliminate the economies with unstable rankings, I ranked the economies for each year from 1960 to 2001 using data from the WDI and then compared each economy's highest and lowest per capita income for the period.[6] Some countries were among the ten richest African economies at one point during the period, but not consistently so. Botswana and Lesotho were very poor at independence but have

TABLE 2.4 Reliability band of GDP estimates for African countries

		Income estimate	Upper boundary[1]	Lower boundary[2]	Highest[3]	Lowest[4]	Range[5]
1	Sierra Leone	410	533	287	9	1	8
2	Chad	429	557	300	9	1	8
3	Niger	486	632	340	11	1	10
4	Burundi	496	645	347	12	1	11
5	Tanzania	535	696	375	13	1	12
6	Ethiopia	605	787	424	15	1	14
7	Malawi	656	853	459	15	1	14
8	Guinea-Bissau	681	885	476	16	1	15
9	Madagascar	706	918	494	18	1	17
10	Uganda	797	1,035	558	20	2	18
11	Mali	892	1,159	624	20	3	17
12	Gambia	895	1,163	626	20	3	17
13	Sudan	991	1,289	694	21	5	16
14	Mauritania	1,017	1,322	712	21	6	15
15	Kenya	1,031	1,340	721	21	6	15
16	São Tomé and Príncipe	1,226	1,594	858	21	8	13
17	Ghana	1,270	1,651	889	21	8	13

		1		2	3	4	5
18	Benin	1,283	1,668	898	21	8	13
19	Zimbabwe	1,328	1,726	929	21	10	11
20	Côte d'Ivoire	1,352	1,758	946	21	10	11
21	Cape Verde	1,777	2,309	1,244	22	13	9
22	Swaziland	2,630	3,419	1,841	26	21	5
23	Namibia	3,637	4,728	2,546	27	22	5
24	Gabon	3,847	5,001	2,693	27	22	5
25	South Africa	3,978	5,172	2,785	27	22	5
26	Botswana	4,269	5,549	2,988	27	22	5
27	Seychelles	6,354	8,260	4,447	29	23	6
28	Equatorial Guinea	7,973	10,365	5,581	29	27	2
29	Mauritius	10,652	13,848	7,457	29	27	2

Notes: 1. Upper boundary of a band of variation of plus or minus 30 percent. 2. Lower boundary of a band of variation of plus or minus 30 percent. 3. Highest relative ranking. 4. Lowest relative ranking. 5. Difference between the highest rank and lowest rank.

Sources: Heston et al. 2006; World Bank 2007.

grown relatively quickly since then. Liberia was rich but has grown poor, and Zambia and Senegal have followed a similar, if less dramatic, trajectory. Zimbabwe and Mauritania have both been close to and sometimes among the top ten rankings, while Cameroon, a middle-income country in 1960, has grown rich since the late 1970s.

If volatility through time (1960–2001) in the dataset is used as a criterion, it can be concluded that only Gabon, Seychelles and South Africa have been consistently richer than the others. Countries that are in the high-income bracket today have not been so consistently throughout the postcolonial period. According to the three tests I conducted using the available datasets for African income, there is very little variation in country-level income that needs to be explained as the outcome of specific historical factors. You may find a correlation for 1960, 1970, 1980 and so on, but the countries driving that correlation will differ from dataset to dataset and will vary depending on which year you use as your 'today' in the regression.

If the problems of inaccuracy, reliability and volatility in income distribution among African economies are taken seriously, there is very little variation in estimates of GDP per capita today that actually needs explaining. It is more appropriate to view the majority of about 30 African economies as being quite similar in terms of income. A difference in relative ranking is as likely to represent a mistake in reporting (as shown in the accuracy test), a measurement problem (as shown in the reliability test) or a temporary fluctuation (as shown in the volatility test) as an economically important difference. Moreover, when we consider that the GDP per capita estimates tell us nothing about the relative distribution of wealth within each economy, the pitfalls of using these variables alone, without other information to contextualize the data, become clear. Fewer than ten African countries can be distinguished as being richer than the other economies on the continent. One of them is South Africa, while the rest are either very small islands or are countries that are very rich in resources and have small populations. However, despite the uncertainty about the meaningfulness of the dependent variable in cross-country regressions – the GDP per capita measure – the quest continued to find a root cause that could explain GDP variations.

Root causes of African underdevelopment

In the 2000s, there was a quest to identify the causes of African underdevelopment, just as there had been a mission to eliminate the

African dummy variable in the 1990s. The growth regression literature that tried to explain slow growth identified a large number of equally plausible but often mutually exclusive factors. Responding to its inability to reach a consensus about which factors were responsible for slow growth in Africa, the economic literature has largely abandoned this venture. Efforts instead turned to accounting for the current distribution of national income levels.

The search for a root cause of underdevelopment in Africa continued, even in the absence of hard data relating to long-term trends. A new concept for explaining the persistence of low income was introduced: path dependency. According to the path dependency explanation, a specific historical event, a set of natural resources, a particular configuration of factors of production, or some kind of 'initial condition' factor endowments led to a particular constellation of institutions that had a lasting effect on an economy. In the case of Africa, this meant that structures, institutions and environments that existed in the past set African economies on a particular development path and that we see the outcome of that path in today's GDP per capita estimates. Researchers have offered a variety of explanations for what they perceive to be the causes that led to the path-dependent outcome. Some emphasize the negative effect of initial conditions, especially geographical disadvantages such as an environment prone to disease (Bloom and Sachs 1998); others emphasize the decisive impact of the slave trade (Nunn 2008); and a third group focuses on the effects of European colonization (Acemoglu et al. 2001; 2002; see also Battacharyya 2009). The literature that puts forward the path dependency theory poses two big questions: which of these historical events or initial conditions had the most decisive impact; and through which channels the variable continues to have an effect. One central debate considers whether institutions or geography are more influential and can be summed up succinctly as 'institutions rule' versus 'institutions don't rule' (Rodrik et al. 2002; Sachs 2003).

Ray (2010: 56–7), pointing to the work of both Acemoglu, Johnson and Robinson and Engerman and Sokoloff, argues that the divergence in income levels in Africa today can be explained by 'situations of stagnation in which the losers (or potential losers) control political institutions and shape the rules of the society. Losers defend an old system – likely one born under a colonial umbrella – and so impede progress.' He argues that even when winners are granted control, 'they may block all redistributions that spread the growth process to other sectors'. In order to analyze causes of divergence, 'it will be of great importance to build a useful taxonomy of institutional performance (and reactions to such a performance) depending on who has control'.

This is an admirable ambition and seems to be one on which some common ground can be reached. Building a useful taxonomy would certainly require a combination of methodologies, drawing on the expertise of economists, historians, anthropologists and others. When asked to explain what path dependency really is, economists and business scholars reach for the famous example of the 'QWERTY' keyboard (as in Reder 2003). This keyboard was developed for typewriters in order to slow down the speed of typing so that the keys would not become entangled. Today we use laptops and touchpad keyboards and could use more efficient designs, but path dependency means that we are stuck with the old, inefficient way of typing. It makes intuitive sense that economic and institutional pressures have succeeded in keeping this particular keyboard version, used to type this book. But path dependency is a rule that has many important exceptions.

The importance of institutions in explaining policy choice in post-colonial African economies was perhaps best illustrated by Robert Bates (1981). His influential model of political economy attempted to explain why some African countries tended to have a policy regime that favored agricultural exports while other regimes discriminated against them. Although marketing boards were a colonial innovation, how they were used after independence depended on the postcolonial political economy. Thus, the theory showed that path dependency via a nation's colonial legacy did not apply uniformly, nor did it last permanently, as structural adjustment led to institutional reform. The irony of path dependency arguments is that they invariably turn out to have limited temporal validity.[7] The lesson is that both the economic evidence and the way in which institutions are classified need to be fully historicized – but that's not how the brunt of the work is being done. In the studies using global datasets on institutions on one side and economic outcomes on the other, the important differences are lost.

The list of suggested historical events, or aspects of them, that had decisive impacts on long-term patterns of economic growth is already long and is still growing. Nunn (2009: 31) concludes that, while 'the literature has made considerable progress in showing that history matters, what remains less well understood are the exact channels of causality through which history matters'. Innovation once again comes through establishing datasets with some kind of exogenous variation (that is, variations that are unlikely to have been caused by policy today). Typically, these include external interventions by foreign powers (where did they come from, when did they come, what religion or legal system did they follow), some kind of climatic conditions (rainfall or temperature), or different datasets on diseases (malaria, sleeping sickness, and so on).

In a review of a book summarizing some of the literature, Nicolas van de Walle (2015) noted that there is now a long list of factors considered to be obstacles to economic growth in the region. One may perhaps still argue that none of these explanations is necessarily mutually exclusive, but that 'by the end of the book, the region's poverty seems almost overdetermined'. Moreover, the question is, of course, not *whether* history matters but *which* history matters.

Initial conditions: bad geography and wrong technology

Endowments, or initial conditions in a narrow sense, are not a good predictor of economic performance. As Anthony Hopkins (1973: 13–14) put it:

> Comparing the natural resources and climates of different parts of the world in order to draw conclusions about whether they stimulated or retarded the economic progress of particular societies is a tempting but unprofitable exercise – rather like trying to decide if life is more difficult for penguins in the Antarctic or camels in the Sahara.

Issues such as the type of technology a nation adopts and what investments it makes in physical and human capital need to be evaluated in light of its specific endowments and local conditions. This context should be understood before any assertions are made that irrational policies or poorly managed institutions have hampered economic progress. When internal factors – such as the design of political systems – are used in any analysis across countries, the comparison must be reciprocal. Pomeranz explains the main principle of reciprocal comparison as 'viewing both sides of the comparison as "deviations" when seen through the expectations of the other, rather than leaving one as always the norm' (Pomeranz 2000: 8; Austin 2007). The problems that arise from a failure to do this are shown in Chapter 1, which demonstrates the error of using a subtraction approach when explaining slow growth in postcolonial Africa.[8] Education, technology, infrastructure and institutions can be interpreted as growth-retarding or growth-enhancing only in their own physical context and only with respect to the relative development level of the economy being examined.

In the methodologies used in the disciplines of economic history and economic anthropology, the question of whether or not institutions impede growth needs to be considered carefully against the social, historical and economic context of those institutions. The optimum design of institutions or policies is not a universal standard, but changes in response to development level and physical constraints; efficient institutions are therefore partly a result of, and not an initial condition for, economic development.

The most famous purveyors of the theory that institutions matter are Daron Acemoglu and James Robinson (2012). Their theory is simple: successful nations have productive institutions. The nations that failed did so because their institutions were 'extractive', meaning that they were set up primarily to extract a surplus for the colonizers. Productive institutions, which were set up to generate further growth, are pluralistic (or inclusive) and centralized, and Acemoglu and Robinson contend that nations fail to develop when their institutions fail to exhibit either of these two characteristics. Yet even when development fails, institutions can persist when they benefit a few elites. Centralized, authoritarian regimes may produce limited growth, they argue, but resources in such regimes will not be redistributed in a way that results in real development because redistribution may destabilize the extractive institutional settlement. This makes sense in theory, but the empirical evidence is built on shaky foundations.

To support their questionable correlations between colonizers, institutions and income today, Acemoglu and Robinson refer to the poorest place in Africa, a place that is also notorious for having 'poor institutions' today, namely Kongo. Or Congo, then Zaire, and then Democratic Republic of Congo. The authors take care to note that present-day Congo does not correspond to the historical Kingdom of Kongo (which was located within present-day Angola), and yet they argue implicitly that the institutional heritage lingers in the DRC in this very discontinuous political history.

Their rhetorical question is as follows: why didn't farmers in the precolonial Kingdom of Kongo in sub-Saharan Africa adopt the plow? Their answer is because of the institutions; that is, because 'they lacked any incentives to do so' (ibid.: 61). More specifically, Acemoglu and Robinson argue that farmers' fear that their crops would be appropriated due to an absolutist king's control of output and manpower took away incentives for them to invest in tools that would increase their productivity. The slave trade, colonial rule and postcolonial regime of Mobuto Sese Seko all contrived to keep this region poor. Thus, Acemoglu and Robinson conclude: 'The interaction of economic and political institutions five hundred years ago is still relevant for understanding why the modern state of Congo is still miserably poor today' (ibid.: 90).

This rather general statement does have some truth in it. The DRC is poor today, and the rule of Mobuto was not exemplary. So, despite the historical discontinuities in the theory Acemoglu and Robinson present, one might be willing to buy into the correlation. But it is generally conceded (Austin 2008a) that political institutions are not the primary factor in explaining the slow acceptance of the plow in sub-Saharan Africa. In the tropical forest zone, including the Congo Basin, the prevalence of trypanosomiasis – a parasitic disease that causes emaciation, anemia and death in farm animals – made it impossible to keep cattle. Thus, without draft animals the plow was not efficient. Furthermore, in most places in precolonial Africa, including Kongo, land was relatively abundant, and therefore investment in land was discouraged not by excessive state intervention but by this very abundance of land. Finally, as many colonial administrators would later find out, the plow is not universally desirable. Tropical soils are fertile only at a shallow depth, and using plows increases the risk of soil erosion. Therefore, regardless of the kind of regime that came to power, the plow did not make sense. And nor does the argument that an oppressive political regime was linked to farmers' reluctance to change to plow agriculture in precolonial times.

Similarly, another issue regarding technology was misunderstood in investigations of the postcolonial period. Paul Collier and Jan Willem Gunning (1999a) argue that public service delivery in Africa was deficient and that this caused slow growth. They use the metric of rural road density to make their case, reporting that Africa had 55 kilometers of rural roads per square kilometer, compared with 800 in India. Noting that there were 40 percent fewer diesel trains in Africa than in Asia in 1999, they wrote that 'freight rates by rail are on average around double those in Asia' (ibid.: 71).[9]

Before accepting these assessments of infrastructure efficiency and attributing them to irrational policy making, one would need to take into account other relative indicators, for example population density.

That road density and the prevalence of railways are outcomes of population density seems commonsensical. The number of users is a critical determinant in the pricing equation and therefore also in judging the optimal level of infrastructure provision. Any data about transportation infrastructure need to be put in a context that takes differing physical conditions and the ratio of land to labor (factor ratios) into account. The landmass of Africa is five times larger than that of South Asia, and Africa has about half the population. In 1961, South Asia's population density was 12 times higher than that of Africa: in South Asia there were 120 people per square kilometer, compared with ten in Africa. In 2000, the population density of South Asia was still ten times higher than that of Africa: there were 283 people per square kilometer in South Asia, compared with 28 in sub-Saharan Africa (World Bank 2002). These data correspond to the data on infrastructure in the two regions, and a similar calculation based on physical conditions (landmass and population volume) applies to transport by rail. Interestingly, in 1980 there were 21 automobiles per 1,000 people in Africa, while there were only two per 1,000 people in South Asia. The rationality behind the choice of transport and technology depends on the physical environment and should be considered before asserting that irrational policies or institutions have hampered economic progress. For some times and some places, building railways is the rational choice. But at other times and in other places, it makes more sense to rely on automobiles.

There are thus a couple of reasons why the type of argument based on initial conditions does not make analytical sense. First, there is no clear relationship between 'bad' initial conditions and growth paths in the postcolonial period. Second, correlations between historical events and income today are too unreliable. However, more important is the fact that many of the comparisons that are used to support these arguments are based on observed differences with no clear explanation of why certain things were 'irrational' or 'unproductive', and without any attempt to demonstrate how these things constrained growth or how choices about how to use resources or the type of infrastructure to build had a lasting impact on outcomes.

Ethnicity

It has been argued that 'bad' policy is the result of narrow constituencies and that this can be linked to a variable that measures ethnic fractionalization in African countries. The theoretical framework for the effect of narrow constituencies relies on work by Robert Bates (1981; 1983), who argued that elites favored economic outcomes that were good for themselves but not for the country and that this was an explanation for 'bad', or growth-retarding, institutions. The use of ethnic fractionalization to measure 'bad' institutions derives from regression work carried out by William Easterly and Ross Levine (1997). Collier and Gunning (1999a: 67) reported that Easterly and Levine found that ethnic fractionalization 'directly accounts for 35 percent of Africa's growth shortfall, and, because it is also correlated with poor policies, overall it accounts for 45 percent of the growth shortfall'. Easterly and Levine themselves reported that 'we find that ETHNIC indirectly accounts for 28 percent of the 2.6 percent attributable to political/policy variables' and concluded that 'when we include the direct effects of ETHNIC, ETHNIC alone explains about one percentage point of the 3.4 percent-age point East Asia–Africa shortfall' (Easterly and Levine 1997: 1235–6).

Note that these regression results do not explicitly or directly confirm Bates' argument. Ethnicity is a poor proxy for narrow constituencies. Bates' argument (1981; 1983) is primarily meant to explain the differences in agricultural pricing policies within Africa as being policy outcomes determined by whether the ruling elites are rural- or urban-based, resulting in corresponding bias. In essence, Bates' framework could explain why Côte d'Ivoire earned more from exporting cocoa in the 1960s than Ghana in the same period, but ethnic fractionalization does not have the same explanatory capacity. The ethnicity variable, which is based on work done by Russian anthropologists who mapped languages in the 1950s (Bruk and Apenchenko 1964), was reshaped by Easterly and Levine as a country-level variable by measuring the probability that two randomly selected individuals in a country belonged to different ethnolinguistic groups.

The ethnicity variable is weakened by its crude formulation. There is good reason to believe that political instability and linguistic fragmentation do not increase proportionally. Instead, it is more likely that two or three equally large groups will be detrimental to political stability than many small groups. Easterly and Levine showed this when they attempted to prove that their ethnicity variable worked: they compared the two countries at the opposite extremes of the ethnical fragmentation measure, Japan and Tanzania. They found that the indirect and direct effect of their variable for ethnicity 'accounts for about 4.1 percentage points of the growth difference – which equals the actual growth difference between Tanzania and Japan' (Easterly and Levine 1997: 1237). While the two numbers are the same, it must be noted that ethnicity has not been ascribed as a growth-retarding effect by any major scholarly works on the economy of Tanzania. While Tanzania is ethnically fragmented, as measured by its linguistic diversity, this has not translated into political fragmentation. In fact, more recent econometric work has told a rather different story. Mwase and Ndulu (2008) emphasized that Tanzania remained untouched by serious civil conflict across ethnic lines, although they conceded that growth remained low. In fact, far from being politically unstable, the government of Tanzania has functioned reliably, if the delivery of public goods is an indication of stable government – in this, Tanzania has surpassed Kenya, its neighboring economy in sub-Saharan Africa. Having an ethnically diverse population has not had a negative impact on the ability of Tanzania's government to perform the basic function of delivering goods and services (Miguel et al. 2004).

Remember that Easterly and Levine's main argument was that it was not ethnic fractionalization itself that directly caused slow growth; rather, ethnic fractionalization was supposed to cause 'bad' policies. However, linguistic fragmentation has a weak instrumental potential to explain slow growth. The only area in which it displays a robust impact is on the numbers of telephones per capita (Azam et al. 2002: 204), a variable that does not explain growth trends very clearly. Linguistic fragmentation has weaker relationships with some of the other variables that have been correlated with policies, such as school attainment, volume of money in circulation, and the black market premium.

Drawing on his own work and on that of Easterly and Levine (1997) and Mauro (1995), Englebert (2000a: 8) found that the effects of what he called a lack of horizontal and vertical legitimacy of the state arising from a high degree of ethnic fragmentation was so important that he considered it appropriate to call for 'territorial adjustment' in Africa. This is a highly premature recommendation. When questioned about the importance of ethnicity as a concept after presenting a paper on the political economy of ethnicity, Collier (World Bank 1998: Discussion Appendix) replied that 'there is a statistically significant relationship between democracy and ethnicity' but that 'we do not know exactly what that means'. Fearon and Laitin (2003) have highlighted the problems with interpreting ethnolinguistic fractionalization indices and have noted that some ethnic divisions fail to be important in some contexts while they gain importance in other settings or at other times. A salient example is the fact that in Rwanda, where some of the most devastating interethnic genocide in recent times took place, Hutus and Tutsis speak the same language. In Rwanda in the early twentieth century, ethnic divisions were not 'givens'; they were created. The labels of 'Hutu' and 'Tutsi' were historically fluid and were economic categories that signified whether an individual owned cattle or not. That changed in the 1930s. In the 1933–34 population census, the Belgian colonial rulers applied the 'ten-cow rule' to classify their subjects as either Hutu or Tutsi. Thus, the state froze ethnic variables (Mamdani 2001). Political identities are sometimes underpinned by state institutions, and that is why political identities need to be understood in their historical context. The scholarship on ethnic fragmentation has taken several steps forward since then, and using some of these data sources on linguistic fragmentation in combination with careful historical and ethnographic work can yield insights about how and why certain activities take a particular form (Posner 2004). However, it remains true that linguistic fragmentation or other variables that are supposed to capture cultural or social constraints do not systematically explain variations in macroeconomic performance across time or space.

Settlers and institutions

One important motive for using historical variables is technical: to facilitate the use of instrumental variables in order to resolve the endogeneity problem that arises when factors that are supposed to affect a particular outcome themselves depend on that outcome. This was exactly the difficulty encountered by scholars who attempted to quantify the effects of aid, infrastructure and corruption on development. Acemoglu, Johnson and Robinson's (2001) seminal contribution was to use European settler mortality rates as an instrumental variable for the risk of capital expropriation.

Before explaining what Acemoglu, Johnson and Robinson did, we need to understand the concept of an instrumental variable. If you wanted to measure the effect of the police on crime, you would instantly run into the problem of reverse causality. While the police may reduce crime, crime increases the police. So, if there are more police officers in one area, there is probably more crime there too. A clever way of solving these kinds of puzzles is to add a variable that is unrelated to crime but is related to the number of policemen out on the streets. Weather could be such a variable. Hypothetically, if it is sunny there might be more police officers on the streets. In a regression framework one can therefore use the effect of the weather on the police, insert that variable in the second equation, and then measure this instrumental variable effect on crime. The ingenuity of Acemoglu, Robinson and Johnson was that they used the historical record to look for such variables that can isolate the causal mechanisms. In their case, they wanted to use the effect that the disease environment had on institutions (through settler mortality), and then use that effect to explain income today (Acemoglu et al. 2001). What they wanted to avoid was the problem described in the first chapter. It is obvious that high income causes good institutions, so therefore to argue that bad institutions cause low income is empirically difficult.

Their guess was that, just like crime does not cause rain, low income today does not cause disease environments for settlers a long time ago. As the man in the old joke shouted, as he passed each floor after jumping off the top of a 100-story building: 'So far, so good.'[10] The validity of this approach depends on all the effects of disease on income going through institutions (and that colonizers shaped those institutions) and that these did not change. It also depends on being able to measure 'institutions', 'disease environment' and 'income today' with some reliability. It fails on all counts.

Nevertheless, through the persuasiveness of the methods, and the strength of the intuition that 'institutions matter' and that the colonial moment was important for Africa's economic development, Acemoglu, Robinson and Johnson have revived the debates on colonization with their two controversial theses: the 'reversal of fortune' thesis (Acemoglu et al. 2002) and the 'colonial origins of comparative development' thesis (Acemoglu et al. 2001). The former argues that the non-European areas of the world that were the poorest 500 years ago are now among the richest, and that, conversely, the formerly richest areas are now among the poorest. Thus, the last 500 years of economic development constitute a reversal of fortunes in non-European areas. This reversal is explained by European colonization. In the poorer areas, Europeans settled in great numbers and invested in the creation of costly but 'good' institutions in the colonies. The second thesis builds on the first and explains the current comparative development levels in the non-European world using an instrumental variable approach. Acemoglu, Robinson and Johnson argue that the mortality of European settlers determined the numbers of settlers attracted by the colony. In turn, this determined the quality of the institutions that were set up there.[11] Specifically, the argument distinguishes between colonies where 'extractive' institutions were introduced and colonies where 'productive' institutions were established – and the latter are the rich ex-colonies today.

As already touched upon, the problem with measuring the economic effects of colonization is the possibility of reverse causality. For example, did colonizers choose resource-rich economies to settle in or did they create wealth where they settled? Acemoglu, Johnson and Robinson attempt to get rid of the endogeneity of those two variables – colonization and income – by finding a variable that does not have a direct causal relationship with income today yet determines the number of settlers during the colonial period.[12] They suggest a variable that expresses settler mortality, using historical data on the mortality rates of soldiers, bishops and sailors who were stationed in the colonies from the seventeenth to the nineteenth centuries. Their argument is that, although the mortality rates of European settlers more than 100 years ago did not have any effect on GDP per capita today, they did have an impact on the development of institutions – or, more specifically, on legal and political institutions that protect private property. Therefore, Acemoglu, Johnson and Robinson feel that they have shown that the *quality* of institutions matters for development today. And because development 'today' obviously does not have a causal effect on settler mortality a long time ago, there is no chance for causality reversal in their methodology. Arguably, it is this innovative way of using historical evidence to avoid reverse causality that has given their article such a high standing in some economics departments.

Yet their method has its critics. The settler mortality data have been subject to criticism and have been shown not to be robust in relation to other justifiable data points in the settler mortality data (Acemoglu et al. 2001; 2005; 2011; Albouy 2004; 2008; 2012). Deaton (2010) warns that those who use instrumental variables often imply that the variable is external to the question being asked when in fact it is simply exogenous. That is, the variable is external to the model but not truly external to the question with which the model grapples. This makes intuitive sense in the example of settler mortality because mortality was probably related to climate and diseases and these factors may also affect development today. For example, Bloom and Sachs, among others, have argued that malaria has direct causal effects on income today (Bloom and Sachs 1998).

The problem is that the story Acemoglu, Johnson and Robinson present is built on the principle that the disease environment, and particularly malaria, was deadly for settlers but did not have a detrimental impact on economic development today.[13] Thus, if Bloom and Sachs are right, then Acemoglu, Johnson and Robinson must be wrong. Let's push these two stories a bit further and think about policy implications. According to Bloom and Sachs, as soon as malaria is eradicated or people are properly protected, incomes will increase and other institutional developments will follow. Development funds that distribute malaria nets are therefore being put to good use. However, if Acemoglu, Johnson and Robinson are correct, the individuals who are cured of malaria will still be held back by deficient institutions, including the inadequate protection of private property. And in an economy with weak institutions, it is likely that the agencies that distribute malaria nets will not be functioning efficiently. The robustness of these published findings on the relative importance of institutions versus diseases can be contested by assessing the coherence of the different explanations. The econometrics in both the Bloom and Sachs model and the Acemoglu, Johnson and Robinson model are internally robust, but any judgment about the credibility of the two arguments, and thus the causality question, ultimately depends on which of the stories most convincingly explains the observed pattern.

Finally, two things must happen if we are to accept the arguments in Acemoglu, Johnson and Robinson. We must accept the use of the settler mortality variable and we must also believe that the correlations between today's GDP per capita and institutions are useful. The final sentence in the conclusion of one of the first articles to analyze the relationship between 'institutions' and 'development' reminds the reader of this problem: 'This paper has not analyzed the reverse causal link from poverty to bad institutions, which may deserve further study' (Mauro 1995: 706).

'Causal history' or 'compression of history'?

A debate has been ongoing among African economists about the value of the contribution made by the 'new African economic history'. Hopkins (2009) offered an encouraging but qualified welcome to the field of African economic history. Hopkins noted that there were some serious concerns about the empirical evidence. Austin took a similar position on the evidence, but in particular raised the concern that, by ignoring time between 'slave trade' or 'colonization' and 'today', this approach was presenting a 'compression of history'. This was brushed away by Fenske (2010a), who argued that econometric techniques have supremacy in investigating historical causal relationships. Fenske argued that 'if X causes Y, this is no less the case if X and Y are centuries apart' (ibid.: 190). A lively debate between Hopkins, Fenske and me ensued in the journal *Economic History of Developing Regions* in 2011 (Fenske 2010a, Jerven 2011a, Hopkins 2011).

The basic intuition of the econometric models that propose that history matters is that historical events have a lasting impact, as indicated by the term 'path dependency'. A social or political arrangement remains unchanged, or even becomes more entrenched over time, as suggested by the term 'institutional sclerosis'. Because the essence of history is the study of the processes of change, most historical studies can appear to be the very antithesis of economists' long-term explanations. This is not because historians are uninterested in causality; it is because of their concern that ahistorical approaches such as 'leapfrogging legacies' may fail to establish causality correctly.

Cooper (2005: 17) suggests a typology of history that is ahistorical: 'story plucking, leapfrogging legacies, doing history backward, and the epochal fallacy'. When 'X' and 'Y' are centuries apart, the probability of 'leapfrogging legacies' increases significantly.[14]

Hopkins (2009) and Austin (2008b) caution that the data used in the regressions in the new economic history of Africa are weak, and particularly so in the case of the historical population estimates in Acemoglu, Johnson and Robinson. Fenske counters:

> These critiques are misplaced. First, the reliability of the McEvedy and Jones's (1978) population estimates is an unimportant distraction. If these are measured with unsystematic error, they would bias the results in AJR ([Acemoglu et al.] 2002) towards zero; using classical measurement error, their results understate their own case (Fenske 2010a: 190).

Hopkins notes that recent work has revised population data upward. But Fenske's response is that the problem could be solved by undertaking 'an additional robustness check that might take an afternoon[,] including data entry' (ibid.: 190).

This misses the point. First, population data are not distributed randomly; Hopkins argues that there is a systemic downward bias in the estimates.[15] The biggest problem, however, is that, by extension, this type of defense argues that the robustness of a historical argument is subject only to econometric criteria. Also, while it is true that the robustness of the model and its internal validity can be tested, using different control variables and running the model using alternative datasets, establishing the validity of these population data is a matter of historical evidence, and African historical demography is worth more than an afternoon's attention.

I think that the point of contention here is whether – or how – one should consider the new African economic history as cross-disciplinary. Specifically, should the 'reversal of fortune' thesis be read as an economic model or as a historical argument? Is it saying 'Let us assume that the population was so and so, and it would then follow ...', or is it saying 'It has been established that the population was X and therefore Y follows'? The term 'causal history' implies the latter.

Fenske shows that the new African economic history is rich and diverse in terms of empirical studies. This is indeed good and interesting news. Furthermore, Fenske reports an admirable goal within economics of 'taking the con out of econometrics' (Fenske 2010a: 180). Precisely for this reason, however, it is a shortcoming of the new African economic history that it has largely sidestepped the issue of data quality. A useful piece of general advice for cross-disciplinary work is that assumptions, data points and observations should roughly match the state of knowledge in other disciplines. It could be argued that this is not only useful advice but a fundamental principle.[16] Economists would be doing themselves a disservice if the only criteria they considered when evaluating the 'robustness' of historical arguments were those pertaining to econometric methods. The most fundamental prejudice against econometric studies is summarized as 'garbage in, garbage out', indicating that the quality of the evidence needs to be proven using the standards of multiple disciplines if the results are to be readily accepted.

This argument extends to other evidence besides population data. Of particular interest is the use in regressions of Murdock's 'Human Relations Area Files' and 'Ethnographic Atlas' in lieu of evidence on institutions,[17] with no comment on their historical validity or their current standing as evidence in the discipline where they originated: anthropology.[18] As Austin (2009b) notes, their use in historical arguments is doubly ahistorical. The observations on institutions in the dataset need to be historicized, not only by dating when the observation was made but also in terms of what is considered acceptable evidence today in the field of anthropology (Bezemer et al. 2009).[19]

A central criticism of much African history is that 'the visions of Africa often derive from Europe and still come predominantly from the Western World. Our perception of the African past has always been a European perception' (Vansina 1986: 40). Thus, when interpreting social and economic change in African societies, it is particularly important to assess the bias and subjectivity of the authors who produced the sources. Administrators and explorers preceded scholars in making observations, and their observations were made using pre-1900 categories. Early scholarly commentaries are also dated. Their racial and political views shaped what type of information was gathered and how it was categorized. The basic question is whether the knowledge gained through these sources is at all useful. The discipline of African history has long recognized these problems, and economists who are seeking to contribute to the interpretation of the African past would do well to listen to the caveats of their historian counterparts.

Bruce Berman (1990) illustrates the problem nicely in a discussion on colonial control and the knowledge problems of colonial administrators. In colonial Kenya there was a need for political decisions regarding property rights. Colonial administrators had unsuitable concepts of property rights and inapplicable notions of 'ownership' derived from their own experience, which did not fit the conditions in Kenya. The arbitrary decisions that were made in allocating land to some groups rather than to others still linger in contemporary Kenya. But instead of learning from the inadequacy of these knowledge categories, scholars still treat them as historical facts in regressions that attempt to correlate institutions with income today.

Arguably, one of the biggest challenges for African history writing has been a lack of quantitative and written evidence. The ingenious solutions scholars, and particularly historians, have devised to overcome this challenge have become one of the strengths of the field. When the econometric study of African economies adopts a longer time perspective, the lack of quantitative evidence limits the types of questions that can be asked and answered, and we may end up with a 'compression of history' as argued by Austin (2008b). African economic data are limited in both availability and quality (Jerven 2010c; 2010d).[20] Furthermore, the datasets are biased in two respects: we know less about economic change for the period before 1960 than we do for the period after 1960, and we know much more about exports than we do about production (Jerven 2010a; 2010b). This means that when we exclusively use quantitative approaches, we ignore or understate the importance of economic change in the early time period and ignore internal economic dynamics in both the early and the later periods. Thus, any investigation of African economic history must both begin and end with a critical analysis of the quantitative data. It must further be supported by a careful evaluation of those data. The quest for a quantitative resolution of what matters in history must be enriched with qualitative rigor (Harriss 2002).

Ceteris paribus: history matters

Despite development economists' repeated declaration of the mantra 'history matters', there persists a serious neglect of the qualitative historical literature and the historiographical lessons drawn from the discipline of African history – to the extent that some historians may regret what was called for in the first place. In the words of Robert Jenkins:

> when faced with studies by economists who use history mainly as a source of data with which to advance unsubtle hypotheses concerning the causes of developmental outcomes, those who had earlier called for scholars to pay more attention to history may regret ever having voiced such a plea, and find themselves revisiting the proverb about being careful what one wishes for (Jenkins 2006: 7).

This concern about 'compression of history' is not only a theoretical disciplinary debate about what constitutes a correct approach to history, it also has significant implications for policy. History certainly matters, but perhaps those cases where difficult historical legacies were overcome, even temporarily, could offer sources of useful policy advice. Just as any political scientist would nod eagerly if someone said that politics matters, or an anthropologist would perhaps agree that context matters, then I think it would be very likely that a historian, and in particular an economic historian, would find it difficult to disagree with the proposition that history matters for political and economic outcomes. So, should we celebrate the fact that economists also recognize history? To some extent, yes. Partly because of this recognition, there are PhD candidates in North American economics departments who combine the use of economic models with careful archival work and thus further the knowledge of Africa's material past. But I would argue that more humility and care are required, and there are some very real downsides resulting from the form that 'history' has taken in the regressions, with global datasets with GDP per capita on one side and institutions on the other side of the equation.

One very real shortcoming of this ahistorical approach is that we draw the wrong policy conclusions. Lant Pritchett calls this the 'Why aren't you Denmark?' policy implication (Pritchett and Werker 2012).[21] So while the intention to begin with might have been 'We think that context, history and politics matter', that is lost in the method when you use institutions as a proxy for 'risk of expropriation' and then quantify institutions on a scale from one to ten. This is the beginning of the slippery slope toward thinking that if one thing works in Norway it must work in Kenya – perhaps the most crucial fallacy in development thinking. Believing that 'institutions' matter and then quantifying them on a scale where Sweden is 1 and Zambia is 10 would seem to be a contradiction, but it has not proven to be so. It is a paradox to be told that 'history matters' and then to be presented with what one commentator called 'Wikipedia with regressions' (Milanovic 2014). Ironically, if this regression literature is correct, it means that global sample regressions should be abandoned in favor of deep contextual studies of history and institutions.

3 | African growth recurring

Different vantage points may produce very different views of the past. Now that many African economies are growing, it is perhaps easy to recall that many (if not most) also grew from the 1950s to the 1970s. In addition, large gains were made during this time in human capital (Sender 1999). As I have argued previously, if it is accepted that growth revived in Africa in the early 1990s, then viewing a decade of decline in growth from the 1980s to the 1990s as being representative of growth characteristics on the continent becomes untenable and the history of African economic growth needs to be reconsidered. If the stylized fact of 'failed growth' is now out of date, what should replace it?

Given the focus on the failure of growth in African history, the October 2012 edition of *World Economic Outlook* (IMF 2012b) provided some surprising optimism about current and future economic growth, especially for areas in Africa. *Business Insider*, a New York-based technology and business news website, selected the 20 countries with the highest projected compound annual growth rate from 2013 to 2017, based on the IMF's estimates; it found that ten of the 20 are in sub-Saharan Africa and another two are in north Africa (Kawa 2012).

In 2011, *The Economist* had conducted a similar data exercise and could declare that 'seven out of ten fastest-growing economies are in Africa'. The exercise excluded countries with a population of fewer than 10 million and also excluded the post-conflict booming Iraq and Afghanistan, which left 81 countries, 28 of them in Africa (more than three out of ten). If the OECD countries are omitted from the sample (these countries are unlikely to grow at more than 7 percent per annum), you find that every second economy in the sample is African. It might not have the same rhetorical effect to say that 'on average some African economies are expected to grow slightly faster than other non-OECD countries', but that would be more accurate.

The 'seven out of ten fastest growing economies are in Africa' has been another oft repeated factoid since 2011. In reality, this is both a far less accurate and a much less impressive statistic than it sounds. More generally, narratives on African economic development tend to be loosely connected to the facts, and instead are driven more by hype. Both *Business Insider* and *The Economist* were reporting forecasts. There is a difference between forecast and actually measured growth. According to John Kenneth Galbraith, the only function of economic forecasting is to make astrology look respectable. According to the IMF's own evaluation, forecasts 'over-predicted GDP growth and under-predicted inflation' (IMF 2014). Another study looked at the difference between the forecasts and the subsequent growth revisions in low-income countries, and found that 'output data revisions in low-income countries are, on average, larger than in other countries, and that they are much more optimistic' (Ley and Misch 2014). Forecasts are systematically optimistic all over the world, but in low-income countries they are even more so. Still, the 'Africa Rising' meme was born.

The perceived novelty of 'Africa Rising' reflected a lack of awareness of the historical data on economic growth. The list of African countries with the most growth has always been populated by small, resource-rich economies. The combination of a very small population, low initial income and rich natural endowments in the form of extractable resources facilitates growth spurts that are not normally recorded elsewhere. The rapid growth that countries such as South Sudan, Equatorial Guinea and São Tomé and Príncipe experienced is typical for some African economies. Other success stories, such as that of Botswana, displayed similar growth fueled by mineral resources. Mineral exports have been important enough to spur explosive aggregate growth in larger economies such as Nigeria, Zambia, Congo and Cameroon. Moreover, if you drew a hypothetical border around, for example, the Angolan capital of Luanda or the Niger Delta, their growth rate would be in double digits, as it is in Equatorial Guinea. There are pockets of very high growth based on mineral exports; if the areas are small and have small populations, this also means that there is a very high average income per capita. In sum, growth – but a very specific type of economic growth – is not atypical for African economies.

Growth is not new to African economies; rather, it has been recurring. Therefore, a search for a root cause of African underdevelopment is not only futile, it is also not useful for policy. Fundamentally, it is asking the wrong question. A basic task of social scientists is to come up with good research questions. When one asks a different question – Why have African economies grown and why have they declined? – one finds periods of rapid economic change and accumulation, which in turn caused important qualitative changes in how societies and economies were organized (Austin 2008a; 2008b). The concept of growth as a recurring process is central to our understanding of the prospects for sustained growth in sub-Saharan Africa. We know how these periods of growth are related to world economic patterns; however, my research on how these patterns change economic power in African economies and the structure of those economies highlights key yet relatively understudied questions that demand answers. Growth episodes have been rooted in trade and the world economy, but they were possible only because of a reorganization of factors of production, a combination of investment and technological growth that had political and economic consequences.

My fundamental reframing of the questions about growth in Africa shifts the focus to the ways in which the proceeds of growth can be reinvested and how African economies can insulate themselves from inevitable future external shocks.

The political economy of episodic growth in Africa

This chapter will investigate periods of per capita income increases in Africa in precolonial, colonial and postcolonial times, using the concept of recurring growth as a starting point. My thesis is that, while factors of production could be relocated relatively easily and producers incurred only temporary social costs when changing patterns of specialization, the pattern of boom and bust had a crucial effect on state revenues. This necessitated a reorientation of states, a process that was often slow, costly and associated with conflict.

A specialization in export production is at the heart of the growth episodes. However, specialization increases risk, and that risk may or may not be justified by increased returns. Thus, in conventional development economics, this is an issue of opportunity costs. However, the idea that risks are higher when producing for a market than they are in subsistence production is not as obvious as it sounds. The historical record is pretty clear: there was an expansion in production for exchange. A rational choice perspective would interpret growth in production for the market as implying that the informal cost–benefit analysis favored specialization. A political economy perspective would take into account the fact that specialization was not always an individual decision; there was often coercion in the interplay between individuals and precolonial, colonial and postcolonial states. African producers have been able to balance these risks, sometimes at the expense of the state. States and their rulers have sought to tax production for the market heavily or have created monopolies of certain resources; then, when the markets for these products have failed, so have the states.

The explanations for slow growth that see a static relationship between 'failed development'. Analysis that merely points out that 'institutions' and 'policies' are less than perfect is not helpful. But other conceptual frameworks are on offer. Gareth Austin, for instance, showed how early choices about institutions, such as production techniques and property rights systems, were determined by the relative abundance of land and scarcity of labor. Austin analyzes factor allocations in the context of seasonal and historical changes and argues that institutions form in response to variations in factor endowments (Austin 2008a; see also Sokoloff and Engerman 2000). Related to this is the staple theory Anthony Hopkins uses to analyze the implications of different export bases, in particular those that arose from differences in factor combinations and 'returns to scale': some production could easily be scaled up to larger operations, whereas other products were produced most efficiently as smallholder crops (Hopkins 1973: 125).

Frederick Cooper, a historian, suggested that we should see the African state as a 'gatekeeper state', because it derives its revenue, power and control from overseeing borders, roads and gates; this fits well with the twentieth-century state, which has typically relied on taxing exports to obtain revenues (Cooper 2002). Jean-François Bayart, a political scientist, locates the origin of this dependence on external markets further back in time. He argues that the slave trade was the first move toward 'extraversion', by which he means that African states 'mobiliz[ed] resources derived from their (possibly unequal) relationship with the external environment' (Bayart 2000: 218). Dependency theories clearly assign agency to Europe in Africa's economic transformation (Rodney 1972), but, in Bayart's analysis, African elites played the key role. Bayart focuses on the external orientation of domestic political elites. A similar logic is found in the theory of a natural resource curse, or the idea that political elites have no incentive to promote favorable institutions when they can engage in rent-seeking behavior based on the exploitation of minerals (Auty 2001: 115). However, Angus Deaton's landmark study of the prices of commodity exports and African economic growth found no clear support for the resource curse thesis. He found that African economies do better when the prices of commodities are high and that they suffer when prices are low (Deaton 1999: 38). Thus, in Deaton's view, the paradox of plenty does not apply to the development of African economies: commodity exports produce opportunities rather than curses.

My perspective argues that the revenue bases of African states have changed dramatically through recurring periods of growth, and that the character of each state has determined how and whether these revenues have been reinvested. In addition, in each state, periods of rapid economic change have been accompanied by institutional change, and those changes did not all look alike. It is these dynamics that call into question the wisdom of searching for a root cause.

As will be illustrated in my study of growth episodes below, each of the approaches I have mentioned underestimates institutional change – and especially change in the agency of states, elites and peasants in the process of specialization. For example, the decision to specialize in the slave trade testifies to the power of African elites and states. From their perspective, it was a means of securing returns through exports instead of taxing land.[1] After the end of the transatlantic slave trade, growth in 'legitimate' commerce occurred in some places, despite the actions of both precolonial elites and colonial administrators; peasants were the leading agent of change in these periods. The marketing boards created by the colonial state provided a way for the state to reassert itself and built the foundation for the postcolonial state. When revenues from this source were undermined by external markets and internal rent-seeking behavior, structural adjustment and a radicalization of 'extraversion' took place. More recently, growth episodes have been based predominantly on mineral exports. The internal revenue base of the state has remained limited, and structural adjustment policies have curtailed taxation through marketing boards.

The importance of economic growth

My focus is quite narrow – I am looking only at economic growth – and requires some justification. It is well recognized that no automatic link exists between growth and poverty reduction, particularly in the short term. Nowadays, more attention is paid to other indicators of development, such as health and education. The Millennium Development Goals and the Human Development Index rightly seek to place the delivery of basic needs to the world's poorest at the top of the policy agenda. In the medium and short term, broad-based development can be achieved by reforming public services to better serve those on the bottom rungs of the economic ladder and by redistributing resources and financial aid. The focus on human development in international agencies that finance development is necessary because it firmly reinforces the view that economic growth is first and foremost a means of improving the human condition and not an end in itself. However, in the long run, a focus on economic growth is justified. Over long time periods, even minor differences in annual growth rates will have a massive impact on the GDP per capita of the country (Helpman 2004).

To illustrate the importance of growth, consider one example. Suppose that three countries begin with a GDP of $400 in 1800. Over the next 200 years, country A grows at 2 percent per year, country B grows at 1 percent per year, and country C grows at 0 percent per year. The results in GDP per capita over the long term are staggering. The power of exponential growth means that country A's GDP per capita doubled every 35 years and is 64 times higher at the end of the 200 years. Country B's income doubled every 70 years and its GDP per capita is eight times higher than it was at the starting point. But country C is as poor as it was in 1800. In the long run, reducing both absolute poverty within a country and poverty relative to other nations is fundamentally about radically increasing GDP per capita.

TABLE 3.1 Growth in GDP over time for three countries with different growth rates

	Country A (2% annual growth)	Country B (1% annual growth)	Country C (0% annual growth)
1800	400	400	400
1835	800		
1870	1,600	800	
1905	3,200		
1940	6,400	1,600	
1975	12,800		
2010	25,600	3,200	400

This simple exercise makes it very clear that small differences in growth rates matter over long time periods. This does not mean that the entitlements of groups and individuals and the distribution of income are unimportant: these issues are fundamental for sustained growth. But when we analyze the long-term development prospects for African economies, the outcome we are interested in is economic growth first and foremost.

One could conclude from this exercise that Africa's current poverty is a function of a lack of growth in the past, and the stylized fact of a chronic failure of economic growth is what has informed the growth regression literature. The limitation of this literature is that, to date, it has focused on explaining long-term average slow growth in Africa; recurring growth has not been taken adequately into consideration (Jerven 2010b), and therefore the scholarly literature has ignored variations in growth trajectories in Africa. By making almost exclusive use of statistics that show average growth over time, the literature has not explained periods of growth and stagnation. By extension, since most poor economies have on average displayed slow growth, slow growth has been conflated with low income in academic explanations. For a scholar interested in obtaining statistically significant results, perhaps it does not make any difference, but for policy makers it is crucial to distinguish between slow growth, low income and growth volatility. Each of these calls for different policy interventions.

From slavery to cash crops: growth in precolonial and colonial Africa

The experience of Dahomey in the period from 1690 to 1950 could be considered typical of West and Central African coastal states, many of which were deeply integrated within the Atlantic economy at this time. According to Patrick Manning, 2 million slaves were exported from the West African region through the Kingdom of Dahomey between 1640 and 1865 (Manning 1982). Like Asante and Oyo, Dahomey grew from a small state to a major kingdom during this period (Austin 2008b: 1005). However, this pattern was not replicated throughout the region. Some states chose to disengage from the slave trade, such as Benin and Kongo, and in other areas there was little concentration of political power (Klein 2001). The slave trade had millions of African victims, but it is generally agreed that African agents – whether states or networks of merchants – engaged in this trade because they were able to realize sizable economic gains from these economic transactions (Northrup 2002: 56). As Austin reminds us, 'Angola apart, the slave traders of Europe lacked a colony in Africa' (Austin 2008a: 1005). European traders generally did not have the means to coerce African leaders to sell slaves (Thornton 1992; Fenoaltea 1999). The impact of the slave trade has been studied and debated extensively, and many scholars have argued that it had lasting negative economic effects. For example, Joseph Inikori argues that 'the transformation of the Gold Coast into a major exporter of captives to the Americas retarded the developing inter-regional specialization and the growing commercialization of agriculture' (Inikori 2007). The direct effect of lost manpower and the persistence of low labor concentrations in sub-Saharan Africa also figure prominently in these analyses. As discussed, Nathan Nunn suggests that the slave trade is responsible for the persistence of poverty in Africa, through negative effects either on state formation or on elements of social capital such as trust (Nunn 2008). Austin points out that Nunn tends to understate the economic motivations for states to engage in the slave trade and has not explicitly dealt with the implications of short-term gain versus long-term effects (Austin 2008a: especially 1003–7). Austin notes that 'most of the African rulers involved sought to protect their own subjects from enslavement while capturing, buying and selling or re-selling outsiders' (ibid.: 1005, citing Thornton 1998: 99; Diouf 2003: xiv; Inikori 2003) and that 'if political concentration had been much higher, the logic of collective action might have reduced the net incentive to free-ride so viciously at neighbours' expense' (Austin 2008b: 1005, referencing Inikori 2003).

TABLE 3.2 Growth in national income and per capita domestic product in Benin, 1800–1950

	Real national income growth (%)	Per capita domestic product (in 1913 GB pounds)
1800s–1840s	1.1	1.5
1840s–1860s	3.4	1.9
1860s–1890s	2.7	3.4
1890s–1910s	1.7	5.8
1910s–1930s	2.8	6.7
1930s–1950s	0.1	9.5

Note: Manning uses import purchasing power as a proxy for national income. He estimated per capita income by assuming that per capita export revenue multiplied by seven was equivalent to per capita domestic product. We should not accept these data as facts, but they do indicate the rate of change and the economic resources at the state's disposal.

Source: Manning 1982: 3–4.

The data from Patrick Manning (2010) extend from the end of the slave trade and into the period of 'legitimate commerce'. A central thesis, suggested by Anthony Hopkins, is that the closing of the Atlantic slave trade led to stagnation and a loss of power for centralized states as fiscal capacity disappeared; this is referred to as the 'crisis of adaptation' (Hopkins 1973: Chapter 4). It did not always mean the end of slavery as a mode of production, as Lovejoy and Hogendorn (1993: 1) have documented: 'At the time of the colonial conquest (1897–1903), the Sokoto Caliphate had a huge slave population, certainly in excess of 1 million and perhaps more than 2.5 million people.' In some areas, such as Dahomey, the ban on the slave trade actually led to an intensification in the trade in slaves in the middle of the nineteenth century (Flint and McDougall 1987).

Patrick Manning's estimates, which are reproduced in Table 3.2, provide a study that attempts to quantify the effects of the slave trade in Dahomey. He estimates that, during the height of the slave trade, Dahomey's per capita export revenue was comparable to that of Great Britain (Manning 1982: 3). This probably led to a rapid increase in GDP per capita, while total GDP might have declined because of the loss of manpower. In the longer term, this kind of economic growth was not sustainable (ibid.: 4). The fact that some states specialized in slave trading as a source of revenue suggests that, from the point of view of those states, the return on slave exports was higher than what they could earn from using labor to produce domestic goods for export (ibid.: 12). The profitability of the slave business thus facilitated the growth of stronger states. For some states, imports of money and other commodities in exchange for slaves further spurred exchange and growth in the domestic economy. The end of the slave trade in the nineteenth century undermined the fiscal basis of Dahomey and other West African slave-trading states (Austin 2008b: 1005).

However, the end of the slave trade also paved the way for what has been called the period of 'legitimate commerce', which is also referred to as the 'cash crop revolution' in sub-Saharan Africa (Law 1995). The shift to cash crops was largely a peasant response, although some crops were produced on plantations. For example, the cocoa boom was fueled by the labor of African peasants, or capitalists, as Hill (1970) calls them. Slaves provided the labor to produce other crops, for example palm products in the Sokoto Caliphate. The growth in Dahomey recorded in Table 3.2 was underpinned by palm oil and palm kernel exports. These growth rates are proxies and should not be interpreted literally, but they do testify to a rapid increase in exports that facilitated growth in the domestic economy.

Less is known about what effect this external growth had on the local economy, and about the relative importance of the external sector vis-à-vis the domestic economy (Cooper 1993: 91–2). Gerald Helleiner estimates that exports accounted for only 15 percent of Nigeria's total economy in 1900 (Helleiner 1966: 7). Flint and McDougall (1987: 398) suggest that as much as 90 percent of all production in West Africa in the nineteenth century occurred outside the cash-based coastal economies. According to Manning, GDP per capita in Dahomey tripled during half a century of export-based growth. Although French colonial rulers taxed exports, their impact on the organization of the economy was modest (Manning 1982: 17). Colonial administrators appropriated some of the revenue from exports (estimated at 3 percent of domestic product in Manning 2010), but the Great Depression and World War Two undermined economic growth in Benin. After those setbacks, Benin did not experience sustained growth again except for a very short period in the 1980s.

The example of growth in precolonial and colonial Dahomey, which experienced export booms first in slaves and then in palm oil and palm kernels, shows that the external market can function as a 'vent for surplus' (Myint 1958). However, what happened in Dahomey was not simply a reallocation of previously idle resources, labor and land (Smith 1976; Tosh 1980). Relying on external markets for exports will not sustain growth indefinitely. The end of the slave trade led to a crisis for African states, but it created an opportunity for African peasants. How that opportunity was seized and how it contributed to growth and development are best examined in the case of cocoa in Ghana.

The cocoa boom originated in the colony of the Gold Coast in the late nineteenth century, then spread to other areas, for instance Côte d'Ivoire and Nigeria, where peasants responded to the earning potential the external demand for this cash crop was creating. In his study of the Ghanaian economy from the end of the slave trade until independence, Gareth Austin writes that 'much of the rise in rural output should be attributed to higher productivity' (Austin 2005: 432). This increase in production of cocoa was made possible by a vast increase 'in the stock of capital in the form of cocoa trees' (ibid.). So in precolonial (Asante) and colonial (Gold Coast) Ghana, there was both intensive and extensive growth, based first on the export and production of kola nuts, gold, timber and rubber ('legitimate commerce' after the end of the slave trade) and then on cocoa production (the 'cash crop revolution' that took place at the end of the nineteenth century).

TABLE 3.3 Contributions to GDP in the Gold Coast, 1891, 1901 and 1911 (1911 constant prices in GB pounds)

	1891	1901	1911
Export production	872	740	3,612
Private consumption of imported goods	1,595	2,741	4,310
Consumption of government and public services	150	490	635
Gross capital formation			
Building and construction	98	837	800
Equipment	56	287	490
Cocoa	4	169	1,573
Net accumulation of specie	73	257	560
Changes in stock of imported goods	8	17	-3
Traditional consumption	9,200	10,000	11,100
Imports of goods and nonfactor services			
Imports of merchandise and nonfactor services	-835	-1,870	-3,050
Net imports of specie	-73	-257	-560
Total A: Including traditional consumption	11,148	13,411	19,467
Total B: Excluding traditional consumption	1,948	3,411	8,367
GDP per capita for Total A	6.8	7.5	9.7
GDP per capita for Total B	1.2	1.9	4.2

Source: Szereszewski 1965.

Szereszewski's estimates indicate a period of rapid growth in the Gold Coast colony (Szereszewski 1965). If the assumed relative stagnation in traditional consumption is not taken into account,[2] GDP per capita in Ghana more than tripled over two decades (1891–1911). This statistic implies a very high growth rate in the export economy and a 6.5 percent growth in per capita GDP over these two decades. In my own research, I put together a historical series of colonial statistics that demonstrated that the growth was sustained into the 1950s (Jerven 2014b).

This rapid expansion facilitated improvements in living standards and diets. Moradi, Austin and Baten associate GDP growth with marked increases in the mean height of Ghanaian people who were born during the period of rapid expansion of cocoa production in the Gold Coast at the turn of the twentieth century, indicating that the increase in cash crop production fueled widespread development in Ghana during the colonial period (Moradi et al. 2013).[3] However, the cocoa boom and the economic growth in the countries that depended on this crop eventually petered out. In Ghana, economic growth ended prematurely because the state taxed cocoa peasants very heavily during the 1960s. (Some of this taxation was indirect because the government allowed the cedi to become grossly overvalued.) Growth continued in Ghana's neighbor, Côte d'Ivoire, until the late 1970s, when depressed world market prices led to stagnation and a decline in cocoa earnings. As Tony Hopkins has pointed out, the economy of Côte d'Ivoire had a slow start because of the discriminatory agricultural policies of French colonial administrators, but then it grew quickly after independence because the new state was favorably disposed to cocoa production (Hopkins 1973: 218–19).

The literature on African economic development has already moved away from a 'compression of history', the methodological error of conflating data from two different time periods and ignoring data from the intervening years. More recent trends focus on analyzing and evaluating trajectories of economic development during the colonial and postcolonial periods (Austin 2008b; Jerven et al. 2012; Bowden et al. 2008). Particularly for the Gold Coast and Ghana, there is mounting direct and indirect evidence of periods of economic expansion and increases in living standards during the colonial period. Moradi reports that members of the cohort born between 1905 and 1920 were taller than members of the cohort born in 1880–93 'by an astonishing 2 cm on average[,] implying a considerable improvement in the physical quality of life' (Moradi 2008: 1113; see also Moradi et al. 2013).[4] Frankema and Waijenburg collected nominal wages from colonial records and used price data from the same sources to measure the trends in real wages. They found that real wages began growing in the 1910s and grew rapidly in the 1920s, and that growth was sustained into the 1960s (Frankema and van Waijenburg 2012). Gareth Austin argues that the expansion in the production of cash crops did not cause a net deficit in food production in the area and that the increase in output was accompanied by considerable capital investment in the form of planting and clearing land for cocoa (Austin 2005; 2012). In addition, Jedwab and Moradi have shown that cocoa production was stimulated by investments in infrastructure, and especially in railroads, indicating that central government and large-scale capital investment played an important role in this period of expansion (Jedwab and Moradi 2011).[5] In sum, increasingly, evidence suggests that colonial Ghana and other colonies were not stuck in low-level growth in the colonial and early postcolonial years.[6]

The lesson from this particular era is that growth was rapid and sustained over a long period of time. Even though production largely developed in spite of, not because of, states, that production was what made it possible for colonial and postcolonial states to increase their expenditures and investments. Meanwhile, most indicators to which we have access tell us that the increase in financial and other resources drove widespread development, including the development of institutions such as markets in capital, land and credit. If we accept the evidence presented, the policy implications are that the institutions were not broken. The subtraction approach tells us that growth needs private property rights and that the Gold Coast and Ghana could not grow under such institutional frameworks. The historical evidence says, on the contrary, that different institutional arrangements can work in different contexts.

Growth in Africa since 1950

What can we generalize from African growth episodes between 1950 and today? To obtain a simple answer, I used the Maddison dataset, which contains GDP per capita data for all African economies from 1950 until 2009, to search for patterns of sustained growth during this time.[7] Different methods have been used to identify and define periods of sustained growth or growth acceleration (Berthélemy and Söderling 2001). In this exercise, I classified growth as 'sustained' if the nine-year moving averages of GDP per capita growth were 3 percent or higher.[8] This is quite a strict criterion. According to this dataset, the average annual GDP per capita growth in the world over this period was 2 percent.[9] I also defined growth failure as being sustained when the nine-year moving average of real GDP per capita growth was less than 0 percent; this is an overall and lasting deterioration in income per capita. I classified the economies that neither grew nor failed during this period as 'preserving'. Figure 3.1 provides the results of my research.

Figure 3.1 shows that many countries experienced high levels of growth toward the end of the colonial period. When most African economies regained their independence, sustained growth became even more prevalent. In 1967–68, half of Africa's economies were in the middle of a decade of sustained and rapid growth. This trend of more countries joining the path of growth was reversed in the beginning

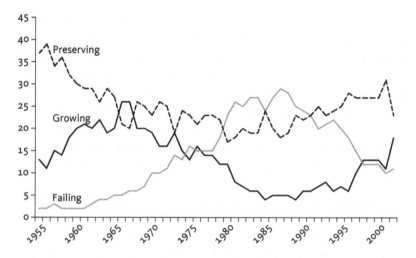

Note: The y-axis shows the number of countries. Whether a country is classified as growing, failing or persevering in any given year depends on the nine-year moving averages of growth. Therefore, in the year 1980, the growth rate is the average of growth in 1976, 1977, 1978, 1979, 1980, 1981, 1982, 1983 and 1984; thus, while the graph uses data from 1950 to 2006, there are observations in the graph only from 1954 to 2002.

3.1 Number of growing, failing and preserving economies in Africa, 1955–2006 (*source*: Maddison 2009).

of the 1970s. After the second oil price shock in 1979–81, only a handful of countries achieved sustained growth in the 1980s. Until recently, any improvement in sustained growth was very slight; however, since 1998, a quarter of African economies have been experiencing sustained growth. From 1985 to 1989, Mauritius and Botswana, which are widely recognized as the African growth miracles, were among the few countries that experienced sustained growth. Cape Verde, Equatorial Guinea, Lesotho and the Seychelles are less well recognized in the literature, but, given their past growth and current relative position in terms of GDP per capita, they deserve the same kind of attention that has been given to the Mauritius and Botswana 'miracles' (Jerven 2010d). Liberia and Chad also experienced a four-year period of sustained growth in the late 1980s, according to the dataset.

Figure 3.1 also tracks the occurrence of growth failure in Africa in each year for the period 1955–2002. Despite the prevalence of the narrative of failed growth in Africa, sustained growth failure was the exception until the 1980s. From 1950 to 1969, only Benin, Tanzania and Morocco experienced sustained periods of stagnation and negative growth. In the 1960s, the economies of Chad and the Central African Republic also experienced stagnation. The growth rate in Tanzania and Morocco improved in the late 1960s and early 1970s, but in this period Senegal, Niger and Somalia joined the group of poor performers. A sudden spike in the number of poor performers occurred in the late 1970s. In the 1980s and early 1990s, failure to grow became the rule rather than the exception among African countries, but even that story was not the same across all economies. While some economies were failing, a number were growing at a modest rate, making progress albeit slowly.

In summary, rapid economic growth and development were widespread in the 1950s, 1960s and 1970s. In this early period of independence, growth failure was the exception, not the rule. After the economic crisis and structural adjustment of the 1980s, the tables were turned and growth became the exception. Finally, it is evident that the recent African growth episode has been less widely shared so far than the boom of the earlier post-independence period.

Prospects for growth

Elsewhere, I have summarized the dynamic of gradually improving GDP per capita marked by episodes of strong improvement cut short by periods of stagnation and regression before growth returned (Jerven 2010b). This growth was based on the responses of African economies to market opportunities, mainly in external markets. These opportunities have made sustained and rapid growth possible for decades at a time. Subsequently, growth has come to a halt because of fluctuations in those markets. When governments were faced with depressed external markets, their prospects of pursuing rent-seeking behavior were undermined. During periods of decline, a destructive search for new sources of economic rents occurred in many economies, ultimately severely undermining political stability and the ability of states to pursue development.

If African economies are to break free from their pattern of episodic growth, they will need to make some significant changes in the factors that have set them on the path of recurring growth. Many variables will determine Africa's future growth path, but the three most important, I argue, are the world market, political conditions, and the prices of the factors of production, which ultimately determine the rate of structural change in Africa's domestic economies. If a transformation in the future growth path of African economies is to take place, one that moves away from a trajectory of recurring growth toward self-sustained growth, substantial change will need to happen in at least one of these factors. Future stable growth in Africa will require either the absence of severe fluctuations in external markets or a change in how African economies are integrated within the world economy. In addition, change is required in the political economy of African nations to enable them to weather difficult external conditions more effectively. Finally, a shift toward self-reliance and self-sustained growth is required. This means building institutions that can invest and reinvest returns from more prosperous times that can then be used to keep economies afloat when conditions are less favorable. African nations need to make these investments in order to benefit from the emerging opportunities in their economies that arise from increased domestic demand and growing factor markets (markets for labor, land and capital, the factors of economic growth).

World markets

According to economic historians, many African economies, particularly in coastal West Africa but also in parts of East Africa and South Africa, joined the 'convergence' club in the world economy in the late nineteenth century. By this I mean that pockets in these regions were keeping pace – and indeed sometimes catching up – with the richest and fastest-growing regions in the world economy (Hopkins 1973; Dowrick and Delong 2003). This period of growth was fueled by a buoyant world market. Although it was interrupted by world wars and the Great Depression in the early 1930s, growth remained strong for the economies that were able to export primary goods for the world market into the 1970s. Some economies, such as Ghana, benefited from increasing demand for cocoa, while other economies, such as Uganda, benefited from stable high prices for coffee. Similarly, Egypt profited from a cotton boom, while Zambia profited from the high price of copper on world markets.

States collected revenue from the growth in exports through indirect taxation. They collected taxes on agricultural goods by controlling domestic prices through agricultural marketing boards and they levied customs and duties on imports. State corporations either had a direct hand in mineral extraction or they charged a royalty on the minerals that were extracted and sold. As long as world markets were favorable, states could collect these rents and finance increasing government

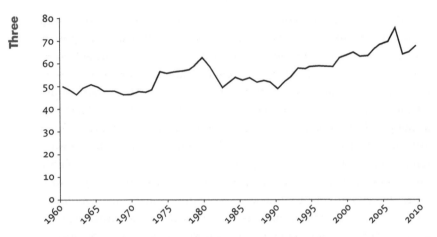

3.2 Trade as a percentage of GDP in sub-Saharan Africa, 1960–2010 (*source*: World Bank 2012).

expenditures and investments. When world market prices fell in the 1970s, this arrangement stopped working. The prices the marketing boards offered were too low to motivate agricultural producers to increase their production. Meanwhile, fixed exchange rates were becoming increasingly overvalued and the incentives to engage in export deteriorated further. Prices for typical African exports remained low throughout the 1980s. External markets improved markedly in the late 1990s, an improvement that coincided with a change in the average African growth rate in the mid-1990s. Over the last decade, terms of trade for African exporters have shown a positive trend.

During this long period, African economies have become more deeply integrated within the world economy and have come to depend even more on the prices they receive for their goods in foreign markets. Figure 3.2 presents World Bank data for trade (value of exports plus value of imports) as a percentage of GDP for sub-Saharan African economies for the decades after independence. Trade accounted for 50 percent of the GDP of these economies in 1960. From 1960 to 1974, the share of imports and exports did not increase; rather, it decreased slightly. We know that most economies showed high GDP growth during this period, so one interpretation is that the domestic economy was growing quicker than foreign trade. The period from 1974 to 1989 is punctuated by the effects of the large upward swings in oil prices that temporarily increased the share of exports and imports in GDP in 1973–74 and 1979–81 (the oil price shocks). The striking feature of the return to GDP growth in the 1990s is that it is accompanied by even higher growth in what is called the tradable sector compared with the parts of the economy that are not traded in world markets.

The rate of growth in external trade since the 1990s is breathtaking. In 1990, the share of trade in the total GDP for sub-Saharan Africa was still at the 1960 levels; however, between 1990 and 2010, the real total GDP for sub-Saharan Africa doubled. Meanwhile, trade increased its share in the total GDP from 50 percent to 75 percent. This would imply a rate of growth in trade of around 6 percent per annum, compared with a GDP growth rate of about 3 percent per annum. According to the World Development Institute, real total GDP doubled between 1960 and 1975 as well, over a shorter time period, implying growth of about 5 percent a year. During this period, however, the share of trade in GDP decreased a little. In conclusion, the growth African economies have experienced in the most recent period is based to a large extent on external trade. If other relevant factors have stayed the same, then African economies are more vulnerable at the beginning of the 2010s than they were at the beginning of the 1970s.

The data series from the World Bank is available only as far back as 1960, but, with some of the historical evidence presented here, we can put together a long-term perspective. The best estimate we have for the external sector's share of the total economy in the middle of the nineteenth century is about 10 percent. This doubled to about 20 percent in the Gold Coast in the 1890s, or about 15 percent in Nigeria at the turn of the century, and had increased to 40 percent just before World War One. This expansion in the share of the economy occurred at the same time as the denominator, GDP, increased rapidly as well. At independence, the external sector's share was about 50 percent. Thus, GDP had been expanding in the nineteenth century, during the first half of the twentieth century and into the 1970s, and this expansion has continued since the 1990s. The period of the 1960s and 1970s was unique – not in the sense that there was growth, but because, although there was growth, the external sector was not growing more rapidly in importance than the domestic sector.

When the financial crisis hit in 2008, most observers, including the IMF, predicted a fall in GDP per capita for African economies in 2010, marking the end of a period of sustained growth since the mid-1990s (IMF 2012a). The dip in world market prices and the effect it had on the value of exports is clearly visible in Figure 3.2. However, according to available statistics, against all odds, growth has been sustained through the crisis (African Development Bank 2011). This is clearly not because African economies are less reliant on foreign trade; rather, it is because their trade is more geographically diversified. For many economies, demand from Asia now outstrips demand from traditional trading partners in the West (Alden 2007; Brautigam 2009; Cheru and Obi 2010). The resilience may also be taken as a sign that African economies were more robust in 2009 than they were in the 1970s. They also derived strength from the depth of local markets. When the oil price shock crisis hit in the 1970s, Kenya, for example, could not rely on help from neighboring markets. Today, the East African markets are reintegrating and the whole region is benefiting from reconstruction and relative peace.

The logic of the thesis that natural resources are a curse ignores diversification in trading patterns and argues that nations that are dependent on natural resource exports are fundamentally politically weak. According to this thesis, dependence on natural resources means that political elites have no incentive to promote development because they can secure rents through exploitation of the natural resource (Auty 2001).

The general applicability of this argument to Africa is weakened by several circumstances. First, many African economies are not rich in mineral revenues and it is not evident how this political economy argument would work in the case of agricultural exports. In addition, the natural resource curse thesis clearly does not apply to all countries all the time: we know that some countries that are rich today have exported raw materials, such as Canada and Norway. Finally, there is a lack of empirical evidence from Africa to corroborate the resource curse argument. As already noted, one study of the prices of commodity exports and African economic growth found no clear support for this thesis. In fact, it found that African economies do better when the prices of commodities are high and that they suffer when prices are low (Deaton 1999). Thus the 'paradox of plenty' paradigm does not apply to African economies – or, at the very best, it is a misstatement of the problem. When growth failed in Zambia in the 1970s and 1980s and growth was sustained during the same period in Botswana, it was not because Botswana was more diversified or less dependent on mineral exports. It was because the prices of copper (Zambia's export) plummeted, whereas the prices for diamonds (Botswana's export) remained stable (Jerven 2010a). Commodity exports provide opportunities for economic growth.

How these opportunities are used depends in large part on political conditions and on the condition of the domestic economy.

Political conditions

Some time ago the discourse on the state and development in Africa reached a difficult stalemate. Since the 1980s, the mainstream view had been that Africa's failure to grow was caused by inept, inefficient and incapable states, and the notion of a crisis of governance in Africa was firmly established. Any diagnosis of states in Africa was therefore very pessimistic. At the same time, however, some argued that the economic growth problem in Africa could be fixed if only (presumably competent) states would create an enabling environment. Both of these arguments have probably been overstated (Mkandawire 2001).

First of all, characterizations of African states were negatively influenced by two mistakes of comparison. States were diagnosed and dismissed as incapable based on observations made during the 1980s and early 1990s. This was a period when most African economies were undergoing the deepest recession they had experienced during the twentieth century, and their characteristics during this period were not representative. It is true that most states have not been perfectly efficient, but it is equally true that their dealings have not been perfectly disastrous either. Herein lies the second error of comparison. The verdict on the quality of governance was made by comparing actual African states to idealized, perfectly functioning states. Of course, African states have fallen short of living up to these kinds of expectations, as any state in the world would. But these comparisons have not told us how serious the shortcomings of African states have been in terms of economic growth.

Several arguments can be made against theories that look at governance as it relates to economic performance. The first is that we know from empirical evidence that states that can be characterized as having 'poor' governance have presided over long periods of growth, both in Africa and elsewhere. The growth performance of Africa in the 1960s and the recent growth performance of China are good examples. The second argument is that 'good' governance is an outcome of development and not a prerequisite for it. Thus, the argument that a governance shortfall in Africa can be linked to poor economic performance has probably been overstated.

Although the empirical evidence from the past six decades shows a clear relationship between a decline in growth and a deterioration in political governance, the evidence is not solid enough to pinpoint the direction of causation. That does not mean that governance and political conditions are not important. However, in a sense the direction of causation is secondary. At a pragmatic level it is of no immediate consequence whether a lack of economic growth causes political disarray or whether political instability slows growth; however, it is evident that the relationship between poor governance and poor economic performance has had a cumulative negative effect. The period from 1979 to the late 1990s can be interpreted as a vicious circle in which both economic and political conditions deteriorated. The essential point is that these are spirals, not traps – otherwise we would not have seen recurring growth. If one accepts that the fortunes of African economies change over time, while simultaneously recognizing that the underlying fundamentals of history and geography for African states remain largely unchanged over the medium term, it becomes more probable that economic downturns drive changes in both economic growth and governance indicators.

It is therefore perhaps better to think of African states as being relatively fragile and particularly vulnerable to economic downturns and temporary fluctuations. The important question for the future is whether African states are more fragile in 2010 than they were in 1960. Political scientists have argued that the low population densities of precolonial Africa and the absence of a political imperative to exercise power to protect territorial integrity in the colonial and postcolonial periods account for the relative weakness of African states (Herbst 2000). Historians have described colonial and postcolonial African states as typically relying on taxing exports and imports for revenue (Cooper 2002). Political scientist Jean-François Bayart dates the origin of the dependence on external markets to a much earlier time and argues that the slave trade was the beginning of Africa's 'extraversion' (Bayart 2000). Each of these contributions emphasizes different causal factors, but they all point to the same phenomenon: African states are relatively weak in terms of asserting their power over their subjects and citizens and their legitimacy and revenues are typically drawn from external rather than domestic sources. Thus, there is some agreement that African states are weak. But has this weakness changed in recent years?

The structural adjustment reforms that were implemented in the 1980s and 1990s were geared toward liberalizing markets and privatizing state activities (Mkandawire and Soludo 1999; Stein 2008). Markets were liberalized because it was generally agreed that state intervention in markets had artificially set prices at levels that discouraged the participation of economic agents. This meant that either producers were circumventing the controlled markets and seeking parallel or black markets for their produce or they were permanently withdrawing from production (Azam 2007). Markets were liberalized in the belief that, when incentives were reintroduced, producers would respond by again producing for markets. Although the response was slower than was hoped for (Stein 2008), the reforms had a direct impact on states and their revenues.

However, post-structural adjustment states have been less able to collect taxes on agricultural exports or duties on imports, and they have relied more and more on financial aid for revenue to balance domestic budgets (Go and Page 2008). Currently, in most countries domestic taxation is not adequate to finance government expenditures. Tax reforms have shown some promise: for example, African states are now increasingly collecting value-added taxes on small- and medium-scale economic activity in the service sector (Brautigam et al. 2008). States that are collecting large mineral royalties are finding it easier in the short term to finance increased government expenditures, but for other, less fortunately endowed economies, increasing revenues through taxation is more complicated. In a nutshell, the problem is the same one that arose in the discussion of state intervention in agricultural markets in the 1960s and 1970s. The majority of African citizens are employed in the agricultural sector and in the small-scale service sector. States are constrained in taxing these groups by the fact that taxing them may very well arrest the growth that states are trying to nurture. In states with a small and vulnerable domestic business class, taxation will have to be levied increasingly on foreign corporations, but this has to be weighed against the importance of being competitive and of receiving foreign direct investment.

The period of economic contraction in the 1980s was met with the fiscal austerity prescribed by structural adjustment policy programs. Unlike in previous austerity reforms, on this occasion the IMF suggested using countercyclical fiscal policies to 'weather the storm' (Jácome et al. 2010). State fiscal capacity is the first thing that suffers in externally induced economic crises in export-oriented economies. A recurring theme has been the state's vulnerability to economic shocks. Instead of being countercyclical, fiscal policies and state interventions have been increasing as economies have exhibited growth. In order to pursue their expansive fiscal policies, African states have to depend on external funds.

There is some reason to hope that future economic fluctuations may be less deep and prolonged, since the majority of African states are now pursuing orthodox market policies. There are fewer opportunities for predatory rent-seeking behavior and states are less committed to large industrial projects to expand infrastructure. What is not yet clear is to what extent African economies will be in a position to soften the downturn for large parts of their populations. Global comparative evidence suggests that states with high levels of openness to external trade have larger governments; this is because government expenditures can provide some social security for the state's citizens (Rodrik 1998). And recent history has shown that managing the expectations and frustrations of citizens is important for sustained economic growth.

A final note of caution relates to the gradual move toward democratization. Two decades ago, democratically elected governments were the exception across Africa, but today most governments are elected. While these young democracies are not without their faults, major improvements are being made according to measures such as those constructed by Freedom House (Miguel 2009). While scholars can think of many reasons why freedom and accountability are good for markets and economic growth, it has ultimately been impossible to prove a causal link between democracy and economic development. It is hard even to identify a clear trend on the continent over the past decade. Some scholars have warned that elections and democratization in fragile states may actually increase the probability of unrest and civil war and that the priority should be on development and on strengthening states before instituting democratization by holding elections (Collier 2009). Democratic rule may be considered an aim of development itself (Sen 1999). Even if it is true that democratization is possible only in well-established and developed states, an overall move toward freer societies must be a positive symptom – but it stops there. Attempts to correlate trends or levels of democracy with trends or levels of GDP are fruitless endeavors. The fact of the matter is that there are poor democracies and rich autocracies in this world. The causal links can not be established empirically; perhaps any such attempt should be thought of as normative speculation on how societies *should* develop, rather than empirical investigations of how societies *do* develop. But there are lower-hanging fruits for economists who go back to basics and look at long-term trajectories in the basic factors of economic growth.

The factors of production

The basic determinants of economic growth are labor, capital and technology. Growth arises when these factors of production are available at a cost that gives producers a comparative advantage in local or international markets. Since the arrival of the 'new growth theory', the emphasis has been more on political and social variables. As we saw in Chapter 1, these factors of growth have received more attention than others because it was found that differences in labor and capital did not adequately explain the divergence in growth rates (Lucas 1990). However, differences in factor endowments are also important. This section reviews some of the basic constraints in wages, human capital, capital investment, technological change and transport costs that were significant in the past 50 years and discusses whether they are likely to be important in the present and in the future.

It has been widely noted and accepted that, because of its physical constraints, Africa has generally been a high-cost location (Collier and Gunning 1999b). Some of these constraints can be attributed to geography and to disease environments that have a negative effect on labor forces (Bloom and Sachs 1998). Historically, Africa has been characterized by a poor supply of labor, while production has been limited by the unavailability of wage labor or by a labor force that is available only at a relatively high cost (Austin 2008a). It has been widely noted that the labor force was one of the main reasons why African economies fell behind in the 1970s and 1980s (Collier 2007). When many Asian economies were profiting by employing workers on low wages to produce manufactured goods for the world market, African economies were uncompetitive (Arrighi 2002). Preferential trade treaties and industrial policies that focused on attracting foreign direct investment for export-processing zones have had some success in recent years, but underlying physical conditions are also playing a contributory role. In the past, wages were too high for labor-intensive industrialization to be an option for sub-Saharan economies (Austin 2011). According to World Bank statistics, the total population of Africa has multiplied almost four times during the period from 1960 to 2011, from about 280 million to more than 1 billion. This increase has received attention mainly because of the challenges it raises for urban planning and other social issues in African countries, but it also presents opportunities. African economies may be able to enjoy economies of scale in terms of their own domestic market and a supply of labor that will make them competitive in international markets. Simultaneously, some are excited about the potential of the 'demographic dividend'[10] – meaning that it will be possible for African economies to benefit as population growth rates fall and the majority of the population becomes economically active, just as Asian economies did in the 1970s. It should be noted that while the 'demographic dividend' can be a contributing factor, it is not a sufficient factor.

Crucially, the productivity of the labor force depends more broadly on investments in human capital. One of the issues of African economic development that has been neglected in the literature is the fact that, despite slow or even negative growth, human capital kept improving in the postcolonial period (Sender 1999). Life expectancy and literacy both increased. This increase was very rapid in the 1960s and 1970s, but there was a continued improvement in the 1980s and 1990s, despite structural adjustment programs that insisted on governments cutting social expenditures. The Millennium Development Goal agenda that has been adopted since 2000 has ensured a renewed improvement in human capital investment. It is well known that the surge in education spending since the 1960s did not yield significant macroeconomic returns (Pritchett 2001), but this may be because growth failed for other reasons and does not tell us anything about the direct relationship between education and growth (Jerven 2011c). Mkandawire has suggested that one needs to revisit the anti-elitist and anti-tertiary education stance taken by donors in the past three decades (Mkandawire 2011).

There are at least two schools of thought about how and when the returns on spending to develop human capital will be seen. The 'poverty trap' school of thought argues that many African economies are trapped in a low-growth equilibrium because the returns on productive investments are currently too low to kick-start a self-sustaining growth process. Thus, large investments that reduce the costs of using factors of growth are required (Sachs 2005); however, the costs have not been reduced enough as yet. If this school of thought is correct, we should expect large returns soon, as human capital has been improved significantly over the past decades. Another school of thought argues that marginal returns already exist that are high enough to justify micro-level investment (at individual or household level, as opposed to on a macro, or national, level) in human capital such as education and vaccinations (Banerjee and Duflo 2011). One corollary of this school of thought is that there are social savings to be made from determining which investments have rates of return that are justifiable and which do not. A second corollary is that the immediate returns from some of these investments in human capital will be low and may not justify a 'big push' investment.

The good news is that Africa has converged with the rest of the world in terms of human development, even if incomes in Africa and the industrialized world have been diverging (Kenny 2005). At the upper end of the scale, African states have more qualified personnel now, despite the effects of 'brain drain'. To give just one example, at independence, Botswana had only 22 university graduates (Acemoglu et al. 2003); by 2005 there were more than 30,000 (Teferra and Knight 2008). Today, African states have a much larger pool of human capital to draw from when filling posts in administration, public services and domestic businesses.

One of the basic debates in the economics of development, especially as it relates to Africa, is whether poorer economies suffer from a capital shortage or whether the real problem is capital absorption. As recently as 2001, a study of the returns of capital in Africa found that capital investment was too high rather than too low, meaning that investments were higher than justified by the returns on existing capital investments (Devarajan et al. 2001). The pattern that was noted in foreign trade is replicated in foreign direct investment. Whereas in previous years foreign direct investment was low and mostly came from Western donors, in recent years many African economies have benefited from capital investment from Asia. Moreover, many countries have emerged as lower middle-income economies, such as Ghana and Zambia (Jerven and Duncan 2012). This means that they have graduated from the category of countries that receive concessional funding from the World Bank and can now apply and compete for commercial lending in international capital markets.

Finally, there are positive signs relating to technological change and transport costs. The most important sector for African economies remains agriculture. However, compared with other regions over the past five decades, Africa's absence of technological change in this sector is striking. However, the lack of capital investment in the agricultural sector in sub-Saharan Africa is not as irrational as it may seem. A relative abundance of land and a relative shortage of both labor and capital – as compared with India, for instance – has meant that it was not until very recently that a 'green revolution' for Africa made economic sense (Hunt and Lipton 2011). For example, the use of improved seeds and fertilizers has been widely implemented in Malawi in the past few decades. There is an untapped potential for economic growth, in particular in food production, in many African economies.

Inappropriate technology and high transport costs have been significant constraints on growth in Africa in the past. African economies have been limited by small domestic markets, high transport costs within those markets, and distances from major centers of economic activity. In addition, because of low population densities, fixed investments in infrastructure such as telephone landlines, roads and railways have had lower economic returns in sub-Saharan Africa than elsewhere (Jerven 2011c). The importance of distance and geography to economic growth is being recognized much more than in the past, particularly the cumulative processes that derive from increasing returns linked to scale; contrary to neoclassical models, returns are increasing with size, which means that the more investment there is in one location, the higher the returns in that location (Venables 2008). North Africa has benefited from being located close to European markets, but South Africa and Nigeria are not yet large enough markets to create economies of agglomeration. Information technology and the mobile phone revolution have contributed to alleviating the disadvantages of location for African economies (Etzo and Collender 2010), but physical investments in roads, railways and ports are still required to boost African growth in the future.

Poverty, inequality and economic growth: some precautions

Economic growth is of the utmost importance for the future development of Africa. But poverty alleviation and income distribution are fundamental to the sustainability of that growth. Some types of recent growth, such as that experienced by petroleum exporters including Equatorial Guinea and Angola, may temporarily increase GDP per capita to very high levels, but they do not lift the majority of inhabitants out of poverty. The danger of relying on the growth of exports in natural resources such as oil or minerals is that the returns on such growth typically are very unequally distributed. This is why equitable investment in agriculture that distributes benefits more evenly is vital.

According to the first principles of development economics, we should expect an increase in economic inequality at the beginning of an economic development process. However, the different paths of development taken in Asia and Latin America should remind African policy makers that this model is descriptive and should not be interpreted as a norm. The growth in Asia during the past decades was not accompanied by a large increase in inequality (Stiglitz 1996). In contrast, there is mounting evidence that high inequality has been and remains a constraint that has arrested growth in Latin America (Sokoloff and Engerman 2000).

One of the underlying factors that allowed for expansion in Southeast Asia without inequitable returns was that economic development was accompanied by successful land reforms. Thus, Africa's current challenge of land distribution and land titles needs to be taken seriously (Berry 2002). This involves more than population pressure and contested authority in land disputes. In Africa, pressure on land is further compounded by climate change and commercial investments in land. The land issue has already proven to be a cause of recent conflict in Zimbabwe, Kenya and Côte d'Ivoire, and it is likely to be the most serious governance issue for African economies.

The relationship between economic growth, inequality and poverty is sometimes analyzed with sophisticated models, but most of the time the quality of the data does not warrant the level of statistical conjectures that are made (Jerven 2011c). In order to tabulate poverty data, you need reliable and consistent data on income distribution, but such data are available for only a handful of economies (IMF 2012a). The economic growth time series data are also too feeble for any calculation of poverty or growth elasticity to prove or disprove whether growth is now trickling down or not (Jerven 2013b; 2014d). This lack of information constitutes a governance problem for African states and international organizations that fund development. In the absence of reliable data on these critical relationships, it is very important for the progression toward sustained and inclusive growth to be accompanied by an open, free and transparent political process. In the end, we have to accept a lack of robustness in the evidence on variables such as democracy, poverty and economic growth and realize that the economic policy that reflects the desires of the population at large is the only one that is feasible in the long term.

The question that needs further detailed study is what happens to African markets and states during the processes of both growth and decline. Because economists have instead focused on explaining something that never really happened, we now have a literature that has fewer direct lessons than we would like when we consider the prospects for growth. As some of the literature is increasingly recognizing, the governance shortfall in Africa has probably been overstated (Kelsall 2013). For policy purposes, it is better to think of African states as relatively fragile and particularly vulnerable to economic downturns and temporary fluctuations (Jerven 2010b).

The argument in these first three chapters has taken the GDP metric largely for granted. It is not correct to equate an increase in GDP with an increase in welfare or living standards. Theoretically, the GDP metric depends on a lot of assumptions – some of which are more philosophically or value oriented, such as the correlation between monetary welfare and non-tangible welfare, and whether an increase in GDP is environmentally sustainable. Even if one accepts monetary gains as a relevant measure, there are more pragmatic concerns: for instance, poverty and inequality may still increase while GDP grows. There are definitional issues too: as an example, GDP increases might be due to mineral extraction or other multinational operations on African soil, and they might be considered 'domestic' in the sense that the value added took place within the territory, while they are not part of 'national' growth because a large part of the value added was captured outside Africa.

What I have done so far is to have another look at the debates that surround the rise and fall in GDP through time. I have argued that, if we are interested in GDP growth, much of the economic academic literature to date either has been misguided or has not been useful from the perspective of policy makers. A third, deeper, criticism of GDP growth in Africa results from looking beneath the statistical surface, and asking what real information does this metric actually contain? This is the topic of the final chapter.

4 | Africa's statistical tragedy?

On 5 November 2010, Ghana Statistical Service announced that it was revising its GDP estimates upward. As a result, Ghana's GDP per capita almost doubled and it was upgraded from a low-income country to lower middle-income country (Jerven 2013a). A sense of bewilderment and confusion arose in the development community. When did Ghana really become a middle-income country? What about comparisons with other countries? Shanta Devarajan, the World Bank's Chief Economist for Africa, struck a dramatic note. In an address to a conference organized by Statistics South Africa, he referred to the Ghanaian incident as emblematic of 'Africa's statistical tragedy' (Devarajan 2013; Jerven and Johnston 2015). I would argue that the real tragedy is not the unevenness of official African statistics but the fact that the then World Bank Chief Economist for Africa did not seem to be aware of just how little we knew about income and growth in Africa. For too long, observers and analysts have taken the numbers at face value, but there is a large gap between economic realities on the African continent and the statistics that purport to describe them. The 'statistical tragedy' had actually already unfolded several decades ago, and this GDP revision was just a symptom of the fact that some countries were slowly emerging from the relative neglect of economic statistics and economic affairs.

Benchmark years

How could a country like Ghana be among the poorest in the world one day and find itself among aspiring middle-income countries the next? To understand that, one needs to understand some basics of national accounting, which is what yields the aggregate statistic known as GDP. GDP is calculated as a sum of the value added by the production of goods and services. The reality is that all GDP measures are an approximation, but in most African economies the statistical offices are simply unable to collect all the information needed to calculate GDP accurately. They have access to very limited data and do not have the time or resources to generate a new aggregate each year. What usually happens is that the national statistical office chooses a 'benchmark year' – that is to say, a year for which they have more information about the economy than they do for other years. The data available to the statistical office for such a year might include new information, such as the results of a household survey, an agricultural survey, or a survey of industry. The information from these survey instruments is added to other data to form a new GDP estimate. This total is weighted by sectors, and then statisticians use other indicators and proxies to calculate – or guess – new annual estimates. After that, the typical practice is to assume that food production changes in line with rural population growth, that the size of the informal and unrecorded urban sector changes in line with the recorded service sectors, and that construction changes in line with cement imports, and so forth. The estimates are made using a combination of qualified guesswork and brave assumptions.

This means that the GDP estimates in the benchmark year are important. Sectors that were significant in the benchmark year will continue to appear to be important even if structural changes occurred in subsequent years, while sectors that were unimportant or did not exist in the benchmark year will barely have an impact on GDP. The sources of data and types of proxies that are used are set in the benchmark year. This means that, even when new statistical information becomes available, national accountants may be unable to add it because the benchmark year used different methodologies to arrive at the estimates. When the benchmark year is out of date, the GDP series becomes unreliable. The statistical division of the IMF recommends a change of base year every fifth year. In the case of Ghana, the previous benchmark was 1993. Quite obviously, the structure of the economy has changed radically since then. In 2010, national statisticians recalculated Ghana's GDP using new data sources to create a benchmark for 2006. This is what caused the big jump in GDP. It turned out that in the years between 1993 and 2006, almost half of Ghana's economy was not accounted for in the national statistical accounts.

Now, Ghana is one of the most closely watched economies on the African continent, yet the news of the revision took most (if not all) observers by surprise. What, then, should we make of the reported numbers from other African economies? The next big jump in GDP following an update of the benchmark year happened with Nigeria (Jerven 2013a). Similar to Ghana, Nigeria has recently announced that reaching middle-income status is a political goal. Since autumn 2011, the news that a forthcoming revision was under way in Abuja had circulated widely; before the revision was completed, the preliminary figures implied a doubling of GDP (Jerven 2014c).

These revisions are of game-changing proportions and have direct implications for what we think about African economic development. While the revision in Ghana certainly invites us to rethink the relationship between numbers and reality, the Nigerian revision promises to change the picture of the economy of sub-Saharan Africa quite significantly. According to the most recent data from the WDI, the total GDP of Nigeria in current US dollars was more than $200 billion in 2010. Even before this revision, Nigerian GDP accounted for 18 percent of the total GDP of sub-Saharan African (which was measured as being about $1,200 billion in 2011) (World Bank 2014).

In 2012, I predicted that the value of the increase in Nigeria's GDP would add the equivalent of 40 economies of the size of Malawi to the economy of sub-Saharan Africa, and I suggested that the knowledge that the equivalent of 40 Malawi-sized economies were unaccounted for in the Nigerian figures should raise a few eyebrows (Jerven 2012b). The next year, when the revision was announced, the increase was actually larger: its size was the equivalent of 58 economies the size of Malawi (*Economist* 2014). This leaves deep uncertainty about statements relating to trends in growth and poverty in Nigeria and, by extension, on the African continent. Some African economies might be richer than we think; if they are, that is good news. But where did this growth come from? That is a serious gap in our knowledge.

How much do we know about income and growth in Africa?

In 2011, I surveyed the status of GDP statistics in sub-Saharan Africa. My objective was to collect information on the methods and data used to compile national accounts. I published my results in *Poor Numbers* (Jerven 2013b). The table I compiled in 2011 contained information on 34 countries and showed that only ten countries had a benchmark year that was less than ten years old. I also showed that, in seven countries, the base year was more than two decades old, and that only six countries had followed the advice of the IMF to update their accounts so that the benchmark year occurred five years ago or less (that is to say, in 2006 or more recently) (ibid.: 46).

In response to my survey, the African Development Bank commissioned a study that provided information on the same variables and published its results in June 2013 (African Development Bank 2013). It surveyed all 54 of its member countries and received a response from 44. However, the report provides information on base years for only 34 countries. According to this survey, nine countries meet the five-year rule and 19 countries have base years that are at least ten years old, of which eight use base years that are more than 20 years old. A second study that set out to replicate my results on GDP statistics in *Poor Numbers* was published in the IMF's *Regional Economic Outlook: Sub-Saharan Africa* in May 2013 (IMF 2013: 6). According to its survey of 45 countries, only four meet the so-called five-year rule (that is, their base year is 2007 or later).

It is symptomatic of the state of knowledge on African statistics that two key players, the IMF and the African Development Bank, published conflicting metadata within a month of each other. Despite discrepancies and disagreements on the number of countries that had recently updated their GDP estimates, both reports confirm that many countries are using very outdated base years. The African Development Bank reports that 19 countries have base years older than ten years old, including eight with base years that are more than 20 years old. In the IMF's larger sample, there are 28 countries with base years more than ten years old, with 13 countries using base years more than 20 years old.

Oddly enough, the IMF (ibid.: 4) concludes in its report that the 'median base year is around the year 2000, which, although now 13 years ago, is more recent than had been suggested by Jerven'. In *Poor Numbers*, I deliberately did not report a mean or median year because I am not sure whether this is a useful statistic. The samples reported in *Poor Numbers* and in the African Development Bank research are both positively biased: we do not have responses from countries that are in great economic and political distress, and we expect, all other things being equal, that such a situation has a negative effect on the timeliness of economic statistics. For the record, the mean and the median base years are 1999 and 2001 respectively in my 34-country sample. Thus, contrary to the assessment of the IMF, my book paints a similar – if not more positive – picture than the data reported in the table the IMF published.[1]

The African Development Bank (2013: 5) concluded that 'overall, the situation with regard to GDP is not nearly as bad as has recently been suggested'. It is not clear what this conclusion is based on. And it does not agree with data presented and the observations noted in its own executive summary:

A country's GDP estimates are only as good as the data on which they are based. Although industrial production is believed to be rising sharply in most countries, nearly one-fifth of the respondent countries had not conducted an industry survey since 2000. Even fewer countries conduct regular surveys or censuses of agriculture, despite its criticality to the food security situation in the continent. What is equally surprising is that Algeria, the Democratic Republic of the Congo, and Nigeria, which are three very large countries, have not carried out a population census in the last 20 years. On the other hand, almost all the 44 respondent countries have carried out at least one household survey of income/expenditure since 2000, more than two-thirds have conducted a household labor force survey, and half have undertaken one or more special surveys focusing on the informal sector (ibid.).

This summary mirrors the view put forward in *Poor Numbers*, where I observed that the main trend since the 1990s has been to give a low priority to statistics about industry and agriculture and to give a high priority to household budget surveys. It should be noted, though, that the African Development Bank paints too bleak a picture of population censuses in Africa: in fact, Nigeria conducted a population census in 2006 (as described in Jerven 2013b: 56–61).

In both reports, the countries that have recently updated their GDP estimates are outnumbered by countries using very outdated base years. The IMF data have the best coverage but may have missed a few of the base year revisions reported in the African Development Bank brief. The results of the IMF survey are reported in Table 4.1.[2]

Arguing about how many countries have a base year dating back five years or less and calculating means and medians on the basis of surveys conducted in different years will reach conclusions of only temporal validity. Moreover, it follows from basic probability that, if members of a group of 54 countries randomly update their base years every 20 years or so, then in any given year a handful of those countries will have a base year from some time in the past five years. What Table 4.1 shows is that some African countries have a GDP estimate that may give a fair approximation of their economic activity, but it is perhaps more important to point out that for the biggest countries (the DRC, Nigeria and Sudan), it has been almost a quarter of a century since a benchmark study was conducted into the size of the economy.[3] This alone adds a serious caveat to the 'Africa Rising' debate.[4]

TABLE 4.1 Base years of national accounts and planned revision years in sub-Saharan Africa

Country	Base year	Planned year of revision	Years between revisions
Angola	1987	2002 (2013)	15
Burundi	1996	2005 (n/a)	10
Benin	1985	1999 (2014)	14
Burkina Faso	2006		
Botswana	2006		10 (1996–2006)
Central African Republic	1985	2005 (2014)	20
Côte d'Ivoire	1996		
Cameroon	2000		
Democratic Republic of Congo	1987	2002 (2014)	15
Republic of the Congo	1990	2005 (2013)	15
Comoros	1999	2007 (2013)	17
Cape Verde	2007		28 (1980–2007)
Eritrea	2004	Not compiled after 2005	
Ethiopia	2000/01	2010/11 (2013)	10
Gabon	2001		
Ghana	2006		13 (1993–2006)
Guinea	2003	2006 (2013)	3
Gambia	2004		28 (1976/77–2004)
Guinea-Bissau	2005		19
Equatorial Guinea	1985	2007 (2013)	22
Kenya	2001	2009 (2013)	8
Liberia	1992	2008 (2015)	16
Lesotho	2004	2013 (2015/16)	10
Madagascar	1984		
Mali	1987	1997 (2013)	10
Mozambique	2003	2009 (2013)	6
Mauritius	2007	2012 (2015)	5
Malawi	2009	2014	5 (2002–2007)
Namibia	2004	2009(2013)	6

Niger	2006		19
Nigeria	1990	2010 (2013)	not known
Rwanda	2006	2011 (2013)	5
Senegal	1999	2010 (2014)	11
Sierra Leone	2006		5 (2001–2006)
South Sudan	2009		
São Tomé and Príncipe	1996	2008 (n/a)	12
Swaziland	1985	2011 (2014)	
Seychelles	2006		
Chad	1995	2005(2014)	10
Togo	2000		22
Tanzania	2001	2007	6
Uganda	2002	2009/10 (2013)	8
South Africa	2005	2010 (2014)	5
Zambia	1994	2011 (2013)	
Zimbabwe	1990		

Note: 'Planned revision' refers to what the new base year was planned to be and the year in brackets is the year suggested for its completion.

Source: IMF 2013: 21.

Table 4.2 confirms that, while Ghana's upward revision was atypically large, other recent revisions have made considerable adjustments to GDP levels. The revision in Nigeria, which occurred after this table was compiled, was even larger than the ones shown here.

But understanding metadata such as changes in benchmark years is just scratching the surface. A country's GDP estimates are only as good as the data on which they are based. As the African Development Bank reports, there is a lack of data on industrial production, very few countries conduct regular surveys of agriculture, and, although half of the African countries have undertaken surveys focusing on the informal sector over the past decade, regular annual data are still based on guesses and very partial information about that sector of the economy.

For example, some argue that the upward revision of the accounts in Tanzania in the mid-1990s proves that there was a spurt of growth after the liberalization policies that were enacted earlier in the decade. But this might be just a statistical fluke. Previous models assumed

TABLE 4.2 The impact of GDP re-basing in African countries at current prices

Country	Old base year	New base year	Percentage difference between old GDP base and new base
1 Botswana	1993/94	2006	-10
2 Burundi	1996	2005	40.3
3 Cape Verde	1980	2007	13.7
4 Chad	1995	2005	6.6
5 DRC	2000	2005	66.4
6 Egypt	2001/02	2006/07	8.9
7 Ethiopia	1999/00	2010/11	-1
8 Ghana	1993	2006	62.8
9 Lesotho	1995	2004	-4.4
10 Morocco	1988	1998	11.7
11 Mauritius	1992	1999	1.2
12 Niger	1987	2006	2.5
13 Rwanda		2006	10
14 Sierra Leone	2001	2006	25.6
15 South Africa	1993	1998	13.7
16 Tanzania	2001	2007	10
17 Tunisia	1990	1997	9.8
18 Uganda	1997/98	2002	10.5

Source: Kiregyera 2013: 13.

that, when the formal economy declined, the informal economy also declined. But today the assumption is the opposite: informal markets thrive when states suffer. Both assumptions are theoretically defensible; the problem is that, because of the way in which the data are presented, it seems that growth accelerated in the 1990s. This evidence has been used to make questionable conclusions about growth in Africa. The economic growth time series of many countries, or the cumulative record of annual growth from 1960 to the present, give the misleading impression of growth accelerations in the 1990s, when in reality this economic activity had existed for a long time but was unrecorded. In the 1960s and 1970s, African states had better access to information because the formal economy comprised a larger share of the overall economy and was therefore recorded. Before the period of decline and the onset of liberalization policies, it was safer to assume that the growth in formal sectors corresponded with growth in the wider economy.

The central problem in measuring growth in sub-Saharan Africa has been how to account for the unrecorded economy. Statistical offices and technical advisers have done their best, resorting to adding a bit of growth here and there to smooth out trend lines over time. Researchers have had to make guesses and projections to accomplish this. They have also made assumptions about the growth of the informal economy, which by definition is not recorded. To do this, they have looked at more easily verifiable growth in the formal sectors.

Thus, the recent growth in Africa is partly good news but it is also partly a statistical fiction. Increasingly, the question of the accuracy of economic growth measures in Africa is coming to the forefront, and since Ghana and Nigeria recently made large upward revisions of GDP, many observers are asking whether Africa is richer than we thought and whether African economic growth has been misrepresented.

I have explained how the statistical capacity of African states was expanded significantly in the late colonial and early postcolonial period, but it was greatly impaired during the economic crisis of the 1970s (Jerven 2013b). The importance of the work done in statistical offices was overlooked in the decades of liberal policy reform that followed – the period of structural adjustment in the 1980s and 1990s. In retrospect, it may seem puzzling that the IMF and the World Bank embarked on growth-oriented reforms without ensuring that there were reasonable baseline estimates that could plausibly establish whether economies were growing or stagnating. For statistical offices, structural adjustment meant having to account for more with less: informal and unrecorded markets grew, while public spending was curtailed. As a result, our knowledge about the economic effects of structural adjustment is limited. More generally, the economic growth time series for African economies do not appropriately capture changes in economic development.

First, the decline in the 1980s was overstated. Second, for many economies, such as Tanzania and Zambia, the upward swing in the 1990s was also overstated. The marked improvement we see in the GDP time series in the mid-1990s was driven by expanding the estimates for the informal sector. Thus, the growth we see in this period was statistical growth (that is, growth arising from adding previously unmeasured parts of the economy), not real growth. Second, some of the recent rapid growth we are recording in Africa is in fact statistical growth that is the result of adding the informal sector and the service sector to the old estimates. It is true that a large part of recent growth derives from appropriately recorded growth in external trade, but exactly how this growth relates to the domestic economy – and more generally to economic development such as poverty reduction – is still guesswork.

Correlates of growth

Is Africa rising? According to most available datasets, GDP growth rates are on the rise in most African economies and have been rising since the mid-1990s (McKay 2013). But it has been demonstrated that these official datasets are invalid and unreliable (Jerven 2013b). Andy McKay (2013: 51) summarizes the pattern this way: 'From the early to mid-1990s on there is a significant reversal: aggregate per capita GDP rose by 31% between 1994 and 2010, an average of 1.7% a year.' An increase in the aggregate GDP of 31 percent is not that much if we keep these other revisions in mind. Both Ghana and Nigeria saw larger increases than 31 percent just due to a revision in the statistical material.

Alwyn Young (2012: 698) constructed an alternative set of accounts based on asset data and found that 'real household consumption in sub-Saharan Africa is growing between 3.4 and 3.7 percent per year, that is, three and a half to four times the 0.9–1.1 percent reported in international data sources'. Young's sample includes 29 countries from sub-Saharan Africa but is biased in that it is based on Demographic and Health Surveys, which are conducted only in countries that are relatively peaceful.[5] The most important shortcoming of Young's analysis is that assets are not a perfect proxy for expansion in income, production or expenditure. Flows of goods and services, as measured by GDP, are different from stocks of assets, which Young uses as a substitute.

However, while this is not a perfect substitute, Young's investigation is still very useful because it draws our attention to three very important issues. It makes it clear that the national accounts may have missed something. This is extremely likely. As I showed in *Poor Numbers*, most national accounts are compiled on the basis of very meager data. In many countries the benchmark or base years for the national accounts are so out of date that they do not capture very much real information on the large informal sector. More specifically, the national statistics tend not to include information on food production or on urban and rural small- and medium-sized enterprises. In fact, in many countries the coverage of what we would call the formal sector is also very patchy. This is the result of outdated benchmarks, obsolete business registers, incomplete recording of the external sector (exports and imports), and a dearth of primary records on economic activities needed for national accounts (Jerven 2013b). Thus, it is abundantly clear that the data sources that are currently available to most national accounting departments in sub-Saharan African economies are not capturing economic growth adequately. In addition, the published GDP per capita estimates are not satisfactory reflections of living standards.

Young's work also reminds us that different metrics may show different patterns and that arguments for using a proxy as a substitute for a real measure of economic activity require a strong theoretical rationale. As Deborah Johnston and Alexandre Abreu (2013) and Kenneth Harttgen, Stephan Klasen and Sebastian Vollmer (2013) have argued, the practice of using asset accumulation and the consumption of basics such as education, health and clean water as proxies for income growth not only introduces measurement problems, it also creates a new composite measure that may be interpreted in a different way to GDP. Increases in GDP imply higher production, consumption and income, but these are not the same as accumulating assets.

Edward Miguel, Shanker Satyanath and Ernest Sergenti (2004: 740) have suggested rainfall data as an instrumental variable in order to control for measurement errors in the African data. As they put it:

Unfortunately, we are aware of no work that quantifies the extent of measurement error in African national income data or determines whether measurement errors are classical (i.e., white noise) at all, although the claim is often made that these errors are likely to be large.

Their subsequent analysis used only the variation in economic growth that correlates with, or can be explained by, variations in rainfall. Their objective was to pick up only the growth that relates to food production and therefore to living standards. What Miguel and colleagues did not know was that statistical offices use rainfall data when estimating growth in the agricultural sector (sometimes for ad hoc adjustments and at other times as the final data). Thus, in effect, when Miguel and colleagues used rainfall to control for measurement error, they were duplicating the exercise that was done to create the agricultural production series in the first place.

Using rainfall as a method for removing measurement errors from the data is a scholarly solution to a knowledge problem. While it may yield some insights for scholars who are looking at particular trends and cause-and-effect relationships, it does very little to remedy the problem of unreliable economic statistics, which is ultimately a problem of governance and the allocation of resources. In addition, this solution circumvents issues of data collection through surveys and administrative sources entirely. A similar problem pertains to the use of luminosity data to measure economic growth from outer space (Henderson et al. 2012; Chen and Nordhaus 2010). Ignoring for a moment the problem that these three proxies (assets, rainfall and luminosity)[6] do not provide coherent, uniform or predictable corrections to the national accounts data,[7] the luminosity data will serve as only a short-term correction to measurement problems in scholarly contexts. In reports published by the UN and its agencies, the countries of the world are routinely rated and ranked according to income and growth and by correlates such as poverty, health and education. It is unlikely that luminosity can serve the same purpose – and even more unlikely that central banks and executive powers will govern in order to produce more light. Moreover, those who are interested in the long-term trends of economic growth in the past face the impossibility of capturing data about the light already emitted into space.[8] Digging into the archives in order to unearth and interpret data from official archives will yield better returns (Jerven 2014b).

This is where it is important to use alternative data sources, proxies and triangulation using poverty data and household budget survey data to make sense of national accounts. Instead of letting one substitute for another, we should engage the available evidence in its totality and refrain from extrapolating these observations to areas that are not covered. Currently, we know too little about aggregate poverty to assert with confidence what the relationship is between economic growth and poverty. The data basis is too weak. Country-level data on poverty exist and allow some analysis of these trends, although one can find better numbers for some country levels, for example in McKay. However, even McKay is cautious about drawing conclusions from the data he presents:

> It is not straightforward though to use the evidence discussed here to draw conclusions about aggregate changes in monetary poverty in Sub-Saharan Africa; the periods covered differ from country to country, the underlying surveys and the poverty lines are not comparable (McKay 2013: 71).

It is important to add to this that, according to Carr-Hill (2013), the household survey data that form the basis of the poverty numbers are biased and miss millions of poor individuals because of how they are designed.

Yet this does not stop scholars from leaping across the gaps in the datasets and making bold assertions. Xavier Sala-i-Martin and Maxim Pinkovskiy (2010) have claimed that African poverty is decreasing much faster than we think. They claim that African poverty decreased steadily from 1995. They did not have annual poverty data for all countries for this period, so they matched GDP growth data from the Penn World Tables with inequality data from the UNU-WIDER[9] World Income Inequality Database. They report that they considered 118 surveys for 48 countries. This may seem like a lot of surveys, but on average it is only just above 2 data points per country for a study that makes claims regarding the direction and rate of change in monetary poverty for the period 1970–2006. In fact, for this period of 36 years, there are 36 annual observations for each of the 48 countries that should be completed – which means that 1,610 observations are missing from their dataset. According to their database, no observations exist on poverty since 2004, so the recent trend they identify is based entirely on conjecture.

The observations in Sala-i-Martin and Pinkovskiy's underlying dataset are summarized in Table 4.3. The claim of reduced poverty since 1995 is made on the basis of data that are very sparse and unevenly distributed. Data are missing entirely on large countries such as Angola and the DRC, and thus the continent-wide trends are based on biased material. There no data points for Angola, Congo, Comoros, Cape Verde, DRC, Eritrea, Equatorial Guinea, Seychelles, Togo, São Tomé and Príncipe, Chad, Liberia or Sudan. In addition, six countries have only one survey, and you need at least two data points to draw a line. There are no data from the most recent decade, and the omissions of the big countries are glaring. It would still perhaps be acceptable to produce a poverty study on the handful of countries for which we have on average more than one observation per decade, such as Côte d'Ivoire, Ethiopia, Ghana, Gambia, Kenya, Madagascar, Mauritania, Nigeria and Zambia, but to pretend that there is a poverty line in countries where we have no data is deceptive. Sala-i-Martin and Pinkovskiy even produce a graph of poverty lines in the DRC from 1970 to 2006 but do not tell their readers that there is absolutely no evidence at all underlying the graph

TABLE 4.3 Data on poverty in sub-Saharan Africa

Country	No. of surveys	Years of surveys
Angola	0	
Benin	1	2003
Botswana	2	1971, 1986
Burkina Faso	3	1994, 1998, 2003
Burundi	2	1992–1998
Cameroon	2	1986, 2001
Cape Verde	0	
Central African Republic	1	1992
Chad	0	
Comoros	0	
Congo, Democratic Republic	0	
Congo, Republic of the	0	
Côte d'Ivoire	9	1970, 1985, 1986, 1987, 1988, 1993, 1995, 1998, 2002
Equatorial Guinea	0	
Eritrea	0	
Ethiopia	4	1981, 1995, 1997, 2000
Gabon	2	1975, 1977
Gambia, The	4	1992, 1993, 1994, 1998
Ghana	7	1987, 1989, 1992, 1993, 1997, 1998, 1999
Guinea	3	1991, 1994, 2003
Guinea-Bissau	2	1991, 1994
Kenya	4	1977, 1992, 1994, 1999
Lesotho	2	1987, 1995
Liberia	0	
Madagascar	5	1980, 1993, 1997, 1999, 2001
Malawi	5	1977, 1983, 1985, 1997, 2004
Mali	3	1989, 1994, 2001
Mauritania	7	1987, 1988, 1989, 1992, 1993, 1995, 2000
Mauritius	1	1980

Mozambique	2	1996, 2002
Namibia	1	1993
Niger	3	1992, 1994, 1995
Nigeria	5	1980, 1985, 1992, 1996, 2003
Rwanda	2	1984, 2000
São Tomé and Príncipe	0	
Senegal	3	1991, 1994, 2001
Seychelles	0	
Sierra Leone	1	1989
Somalia	1	2002
South Africa	3	1993, 1997, 2000
Sudan	0	
Swaziland	2	1994, 2001
Tanzania	3	1992, 1993, 2001
Togo	0	
Tunisia	4	1970, 1985, 1990, 2000
Uganda	3	1970, 1992, 2000
Zambia	5	1976, 1991, 1993, 1996, 1998
Zimbabwe	2	1990, 1995

Note: This is based on the metadata of the data extracted from the UNU-WIDER World Income Inequality Database by Sala-i-Martin and Pinkovskiy.

(ibid.: Figure 10). This empirical part of the study is just pretense, because the graph has no relation to the real world.

There seems to be considerable pressure on scholars and international organizations to supply continent-wide statements on poverty, growth and the quality of institutions, because, although seldom defensible, continent-wide trends are provided. A recurring theme is that in numerous recent studies that purport to portray continent-wide data – whether it be data on corruption or data on inequality – a few observations from some African countries have been used to stand in for actual country observations. The use of data from the Demographic and Health Surveys by Alwyn Young mentioned earlier also suffers from this bias. In some cases, claims of a rising middle class in Africa between 1990 and 2011 have been made although the data contain only 84 observations from 35 countries and there are more than 1,000 gaps in the country time series (Ncube and Shimeles 2013). Authors of reports such as the IMF's *Regional Economic Outlook* find themselves in a similar predicament when they release growth data for very recent years: the data are not yet produced by many, if not most, countries. Various methods are being used to fill the holes in the databases, but simultaneously our knowledge gap on poverty and growth in Africa is increasing.

Interpreting the growth evidence

It is likely that very recent growth data are overestimating economic growth. First, for some economies – and Ghana is the best example – the growth figures are higher because there was a recent large upward revision in GDP levels. When the time series is smoothed out across the 2000s in light of these new data, it shows an exaggerated acceleration in growth. Second, for those economies that have very outdated base years, the GDP level is most probably underestimated. This has two effects. One is obvious: when the base is too low, growth estimates are too high. One of the key reasons a comprehensive GDP estimate is desirable is to avoid statistical growth. A second effect results from statisticians and consultants adding to the GDP measure to make it more exhaustive by revising current and previous GDP estimates upward as they go along. When it is obvious that GDP has been underestimated, it makes sense to add some growth to the estimates in order to produce a more representative GDP. It may also be in the interests of the statistical office to preempt a large future upward revision (particularly when some data sources become available before the revision is complete, as in the cases of Nigeria and Ghana) by gradually adjusting recent and earlier GDP estimates upward. There is a conflict between two aims – reliability and validity. Validity refers to whether the GDP estimate is correct, or exhaustive, whereas reliability refers to whether the measurement is predictable. Efforts to make estimates more valid may cause problems for data users who are interested in a reliable measure of economic growth but not necessarily in a correct level of GDP. According to Alan Heston (1994: 37): 'Often officials, who use national accounts for growth purposes and who also evaluate work programs of statistical offices, may resist improvements in level estimates of output because it will introduce breaks in national accounts series.' Recent economic growth is probably overstated for countries that have recently or are currently undertaking a GDP revision. For those countries that have not yet undertaken such a revision, there is also an effect that biases the estimates of growth upward: the size of the economy is small, and therefore large impacts on GDP derive from external change that, at present, is proportionally too large.

Quite a bit of the recent economic growth in Africa is not grounded in observed or recorded economic change but rather is simply based on an assumption. Because there is some growth in the formally recorded sector, accountants assume that growth in the informal sector is also increasing, and they adjust the GDP estimates to capture growth in those unrecorded areas. Predictions about what will happen in the economy of South Sudan provide a good example of how reported economic growth can bear little relation to what is happening in an economy. According to the *World Economic Outlook* for 2012, the economy that was projected to grow most rapidly in 2013 was that of South Sudan, at a growth rate of 69.62 percent. But in that same report, which economy was projected to grow most slowly in 2012? Answer: South Sudan again – this time at minus 54.98 percent. It might be tempting to write this off as miscalculations at the world's youngest statistical office, but these data are probably more or less right. Of course, not to the second decimal point, and maybe give or take 5 or 10 percent, but economic growth in South Sudan depends on the flow of petroleum, which was hindered in 2012 but projected to flow freely in 2013.

South Sudan is an extreme example, but, by and large, the growth data are driven by changes in the petroleum sector. Added to this is the fact that we have little or no information on economic growth in the informal sector. Take the example of Ghana. In the survey data used by the Ghana Statistical Service to update the nation's statistics for the new base year of 2006, there was some information on previously unrecorded economic activities. But after 2006 there is no information on the informal sector. Economic growth in Ghana's now very large and important small-scale service sector is primarily driven by data on value-added taxes, but, by definition, those statistics do not include the informal sector.[10] The situation is similar in other countries. Changes to and revisions of GDP base years will cause big jumps and ad hoc improvements, but GDP growth data require reliable annual figures over a period of years. Changes in the national accounts are driven by changes in the formal sector and often in the external sector. Therefore, when observers (such as Lipton 2012) say that growth in the national

119

accounts is driven mainly by mining and does not reflect changes in labor productivity or agricultural yields, they are mostly right.

What has been described here is a considerable knowledge problem. Currently, there are serious difficulties in the regular collection of economic statistics. Statistical offices lack funding and other resources and face bureaucratic challenges that undermine regular access to and provision of the necessary primary data. Our current estimates are doubly biased: we know less about the economies that are poorer than we do about those that are wealthier, and we know less about the populations that are poor in those poor economies than we do about the populations of the wealthier countries. This knowledge problem stands in striking contrast to the demand for numbers in the development community. In macro-analyses of growth and poverty, the distance between the observed and the observer has grown since the 1990s, as analysts have increasingly made use of downloadable datasets to test econometric models. There needs to be a change of practice toward more carefully conducted country case studies, and the statements about 'Africa Rising' need to be viewed with some caution.

So what do the recent and previous episodes of economic growth mean, and why should we not ignore them? There is no doubt that there has been an expansion in recorded exports and imports, an increase in investment in physical capital, and growth in the capacity to extract natural resources. More goods and services are entering and leaving the continent today than a decade ago. However, claims of an increase in GDP are more problematic. There are many gaps in the data, the claim is overstated, and there are large blind spots in the data that mislead scholars.

The GDP numbers should not be interpreted as proof of changes in living standards, nor are they good metrics of increases in productivity. The data on personal expenditure and on labor productivity in the agricultural and informal sector are far too weak to draw such implications. Most of the time the econometric methods are far more sophisticated than the data they are supposed to explain. However, the data do tell us something: they tell us that there has been expansion in the formal, modern and external sectors. We do not know how this expansion relates to the unobserved (informal) economy, but we know that states are able to take advantage of growth in formal and recorded growth. This means that there is change and that there are opportunities for further change. This is why this current period of growth should not be ignored: it should be seized upon to secure future growth on the African continent.

The politics of African economic statistics

I have argued that African countries have been slowly emerging from the relative neglect of economic statistics and economic affairs in the past decade, and that these big jumps in GDP we have observed in Ghana, Nigeria, Zambia, Uganda, Tanzania and elsewhere are just indications that both external observers and domestic leaders are suddenly prioritizing and recognizing the importance of economic performance.

I have noticed this gradual change on a personal level. When I undertook my PhD fieldwork on the measurement of economic activities and how it mattered for economic growth and I visited statistical offices in the region between 2007 and 2011, no one was really interested. Things changed when the 'Africa Rising' narrative became dominant. When *Poor Numbers* was published in 2013, the book was reviewed by the *Financial Times* under the heading 'Africa counts the cost of miscalculations' (Jack 2013). The potential cost of that title in terms of a loss of investments or having to pay higher risk premiums on loans and bonds prompted a response. In the case of the African Development Bank, I think some individuals were concerned that if too many questions were asked about the accuracy of the GDP numbers, then this might have a negative effect on the decisions of investors. And they were right – during this period I received frequent calls from investment banks that wanted to know how big Nigeria's GDP really was.

In response to the review of *Poor Numbers* in the *Financial Times*, Mthuli Ncube, Chief Economist and Vice President of the African Development Bank Group, wrote to the newspaper to say that Africa's rise was real, and despite the uncertainty surrounding the numbers, 'For investors, for visitors, for Africans themselves, seeing is believing. The growth is tangible. Come and see for yourself.'[11] Of course, I am somewhat sympathetic to his position. However, one reason why we produce statistics is in order to be able to make informed decisions about the magnitude and pace of economic growth rather than having to rely on subjective impressions from visitors. Without these statistics it is impossible to properly analyze the distribution of income or the growth effect on poverty.

The question of the reliability of the statistics was addressed in the reports of international organizations. As we have seen, the IMF's

Regional Economic Outlook reports for Africa, as well as the United Nations Economic Commission for Africa (UNECA) and the African Development Bank, carried out replication studies of my information on the comparable statistics for African countries. The African Development Bank report spent most of its time responding to the stories in the media, but also found fundamentally the same picture when it came to describing the current situation with regard to the provision of economic statistics.

But the response was not always polite and was not always limited to collegial replication studies; some officials in statistical offices in the region felt personally aggrieved, to the extent that the Zambia Statistical Office accused me of being 'a hired gun meant to discredit African National Accountants and eventually create work and room for more European-based technical assistance missions' (as reported in Taylor 2013). It was disappointing to see that the public exchange fell to such a low level. Then, in 2013, I was supposed to give a talk at UNECA in Addis Ababa, but while I was on my way there I was notified that the General Statistician in South Africa had intervened to have my talk cancelled.[12] The fallout from that event prompted the *Financial Times* to comment on the debate on African statistics in an editorial with the heading 'Africa at dawn':

> Too often, the continent's leaders have punished western scholars for questioning government numbers. Critical voices have even been ex-cluded from regional economic forums by means of informal bans.[13]

Ultimately, attempts to silence debate are futile, and while the statistical leaders in South Africa and Zambia thought that their attempt was wise, many other statistical offices were willing to communicate openly and freely (Jerven et al. 2015). The legitimacy of official statistics in studies of African economies is easy to gauge. In the 1970s and 1980s, careful country studies used to be the norm, and they included references to the statistical offices and their published statistical abstracts or external trade statistics. Since the 1990s, any similar study would hesitate to rely on official statistics but would be happy to use 'international' information such as the WDI, although the actual numbers are the same. It is a matter of legitimacy and authority, not an issue of whether or not the numbers relate to the reality. This increasing distance between the observer and the observed in the study of macroeconomics in Africa is worrying. The careful study of economies has given way to cross-country growth regressions with global datasets. With downloaded data, there are few ways of double-checking whether reality and the datasets correspond.

When confronted with an observation – for example a growth projection that underlies a statement such as 'seven out of the ten fastest growing economies are in Africa' or 'Africa Rising' – the role of scholarly research is to ask what kind of knowledge these statements are based on. It is frustrating that the narratives in African economic development switch from one extreme to the other so swiftly. Of course, the truth lies somewhere between the 'miracles' and 'tragedies'. We went from 'Bottom Billion' to 'Africa Rising' within half a decade. So while there is no doubt that there are more goods leaving and entering the African continent today than there were 15 years ago, and there surely are more roads and hotels being built and more capital flowing in and out of Africa than before, questions still remain. What is the real pace of economic growth? Does the increase in the volume of transactions result in a sustained increase in living standards? As yet, the evidence does not readily provide us with an answer. It is the job of scholars to give tempered assessments that navigate between what is make-believe and what passes as plausible evidence. That's how you avoid a statistical tragedy.

Conclusion

There has been a chronic failure among economists to explain growth in Africa. The following question arises: do economists have a character flaw that makes them incapable of doing good scholarly work on Africa? Economists certainly became trapped in history. The methods and analytical angles they have used to explain relative failure in Africa were conceived in the 1990s, but these methods were unsuitable for explaining growth in the 1960s or growth since the 2000s.

Yet the economists studying poverty and growth in Africa were path-dependent and destined to fail. The econometricians suffered from difficult initial conditions and unsuitable factor endowments. Many were intellectually 'landlocked with bad neighbors'. Reliant on econometric models and downloads from international databases, they suffered from poor access to the ocean of real-world data. These poor initial conditions and unfortunate intellectual legacies explain in part why economists fail.

The outcome of these two lost decades leaves us very little guidance on how to analyze, let alone explain, current economic trends in Africa. At the moment, we are unable to explain why African nations fail, why they are poor, why they grow slowly, and why they adopt poor policies and are trapped in poverty with bad institutions. What we cannot explain is how African economies are growing or why they are growing, and there is no reliable policy advice on offer.

How we are misled by mainstream economics

I have laid out the origins of the mistake in this book. There is no denying that there was an economic failure in many African economies and that this decline took place during the postcolonial period. But it did not coincide with the *whole* period. 'Postcolonial period' and 'economic failure' should not be equated, but they have been in the literature that attempts to explain growth in postcolonial Africa. This erroneous stylized fact provided the impetus for a literature that compressed a history that moved from explaining the African growth shortfall to explaining the gap in GDP per capita between African economies and the rich countries in the rest of the world.

I have shown how dispensing with the average growth outcome perspective changes the way in which the postcolonial growth record is both narrated and explained. This is because, by doing this, we are provided with an insight into periods of growth. When those periods become visible, it suddenly stops seeming at all plausible that initial conditions such as 'high' ethnic fragmentation and measures of 'low' social capital had a direct role in the failure of economic growth in the late 1970s. At best, there may have been some latent factors, but the causality story – initial conditions causing slow growth – is wrong and therefore not useful for policy advice. Moreover, policy typologies such as the distinction between 'closed' and 'open' economies, or the related 'bad' and 'good' policies, do not correlate coherently with episodes of economic growth in African countries.

The regression literature on African economic growth has inflated the narrative of economic failure, applying it to the whole period and then falsely blaming economic policy and institutional arrangements. I have shown that these 'bad' policies and 'institutions' could manifestly coexist with sustained economic progress. The fact that these periods of economic growth were not sustained indefinitely does not mean that there were no lasting effects. Gains were made in infrastructure development and human capital that have not been reversed.

Africa's growth failure happened because of a combination of external economic shocks and a less-than-perfect policy response, from both international donors and national economic policy makers. But laying the blame solely on institutions and policies was a costly mistake. Cause and effect were reversed in the growth literature, and several decades were wasted putting a lot of effort into curing symptoms that were thought to be causes. If structural adjustment had been conceived as a policy package that was intended to remedy the effects of economic decline, it would have been more successful. Instead, structural adjustment policies were misguided.

Another important consequence of the quest for the African dummy variable is that being 'African' has emerged in the literature as a potentially explanatory factor. It was forgotten that there is at least as much to explain in terms of diversity in economic performance and growth characteristics *within* Africa as there is between Africa and the rest of the world. It is not appropriate to treat Africa as if it consists of a collection of homogeneous experiences.

All African economies have experienced the fluctuations and

contractions of world markets, but different economies had different levels of exposure to world markets and they put different policies in place to manage their interactions with those markets. The development of world markets after 1973 was bad news for all African economies except the petroleum-exporting ones. Dependence on world markets for primary commodity exports led to a convergence of negative economic performance in the 1980s, with only a few exceptions. This convergence in economic performance paved the way for a convergence in policy advice, as African economies embarked on relatively homogeneous structural adjustment programs that were not suited to heterogeneous country conditions.

It seems crucial that we understand the heterogeneity of African economies, especially in terms of political economy and policy priorities before structural adjustment. The differences in political economy might help explain why certain economies prioritized exports of cash crops while others did not. Robert Bates (1981) has illustrated this by, for example, juxtaposing Kenya with Tanzania, which had a bias against agricultural exports. In Kenya, the elites had vested interests in coffee, in Tanzania they did not, and Bates argues that this may help explain some policy choices. Such policy differences are not picked up by simple variables such as ethnicity or by other quantitative parameters. Both economies ran into external market problems in the 1980s for similar reasons, which led to a convergence in policy advice in the 1990s. These changes, nuances and trajectories cannot be explained satisfactorily or recognized in cross-country regressions. The regression literature often refers to anecdotal evidence to support and confirm the use of certain variables in the model specification. It is testament to the diversity of country experiences and characteristics within Africa that it is always easy to find a country that provides a story that will prove or disprove the general validity of the causal relationships on offer.

More generally, the fact that the states that most analysts characterize as having 'poor governance' have presided over long periods of growth, both in Africa and elsewhere, is a strong argument against the claim that political governance, as defined in the mainstream literature, is a determining factor in economic history. Africa's growth performance in the 1960s and China's recent growth performance are good examples. A second argument against the link between governance styles and economic performance is the fact that 'good governance' is an outcome of development and not a prerequisite for growth. A government's capacity to make changes in response to levels of development and physical constraints is in part a result of – and not an initial condition for – economic development.

Institutional quality has become the all-embracing variable for explaining divergence in economic growth. If one is willing to accept two propositions put forward by a 'subtraction approach', then looking for correlations between GDP per capita and institutional indexes makes little sense. The first proposition is that 'late development' will differ considerably from the way in which already developed countries grew because of differences in institutional frameworks (Gerschenkron 1962). The second follows from the first – the concept that there is no general list of prerequisites for growth and that we cannot distinguish such prerequisites from the 'final' result of development. Efficient institutions may be a characteristic of a well-functioning and developed economy, but they are hardly the cause. These propositions are in conflict with the underlying assumptions of exercises like the one conducted by Kaufmann and colleagues (1999), where institutional quality was used as an indicator, with assigned values ranging from –2.5 to 2.5; perfect institutions scored 2.5 and the worst –2.5, as if the same institutions were appropriate for all countries. Here, a 'one size fits all' perspective finds its highest level. A brief summary of successful development experiences in the twentieth century would inform us that there is no such thing as 'one size fits all'. The best practice paradigm is a fallacy, not only because of the presence of informal institutions, as Douglass North (1990) argues, but also in two other ways. First, the optimal design of institutions is not an absolute but changes in response to development level. Thus, efficient institutions are a result of – and not an initial condition for – economic development. Second, assessments of the potential for growth and of the factors that constrain growth in any economy should look at economic development within a historical context and should compare a given economy's experience with those of nearby economies. Only then can we understand why certain decisions were made and why some institutions were strengthened while others were not. The subtraction approach will not yield this level of knowledge because it starts with an external standard. We need to understand the history of economic development from a perspective that comes from internal conditions and knowledge.

Learning from history

In order to assess the future, we need an accurate picture of the past. History is unlikely to repeat itself, but the past should not be dismissed as a failure of growth. There is much to learn from the periods of growth and stagnation. It is quite obvious that future growth will depend on a multitude of variables, and that accurate projections are not feasible. However, it is also beyond doubt that world markets, local political conditions and the costs of factors of production in the domestic economy will play a large part in determining future growth trajectories. To predict the growth of the world economy is a tall order. Our best guess is that markets will continue to fluctuate, as they have done in the past. But this will not mean more of the same for Africa. African economies' integration into the world economy has changed. In particular, the rise of Asia has diversified the pattern of geographical dependency for many African economies, giving a reason to hope that Africa's continued dependence on external markets will not result in the same type of volatility the continent has experienced in the past.

But economic development is about more than just institutions. The fundamentals of economic growth still matter, and they can explain more than is commonly thought in the literature today. Increases in production and productivity result from a combination of labor, capital and technology. In the past, labor in Africa (particularly in sub-Saharan Africa) has been relatively scarce and therefore expensive. Levels of human capital (health and education) in Africa have been relatively low compared with the situation in other regions, even though changes in human capital have been reasonably significant over the past 50 years or so. Moreover, even though Africa has had a shortage of capital, it has received less in international capital flows than other regions. Finally, technology is crucial. In general, the cutting edge of technological change around the world has been dominated by two trends. Some capital-intensive technologies are intended to substitute for labor. These have reaped major benefits in areas where the cost of labor is relatively high, such as Europe and North America. Other new production techniques have been geared toward taking advantage of a large supply of labor and low wages, a path to which Asian economies have successfully adapted. Neither of these sets of conditions is relevant in Africa. The markets in Africa are characterized by both a short supply of labor and low wages. In sum, the technological innovations of the twentieth century have not been suitable for African economies – and therefore they have not been readily adapted.

African economies had a locational disadvantage in the twentieth century. Thanks to improvements in technology, transport costs decreased significantly over the past century, but there is considerable evidence that sub-Saharan Africa, especially the landlocked countries, has suffered from the high costs of distance from world markets. In the past, transport and communication technologies typically relied on large investments in fixed infrastructure, such as telephone lines and railways. But because of the low ratio of population to land, these investments have had lower returns in sub-Saharan Africa than they have had elsewhere. In the agricultural sector, Africa experienced a long-lasting boom from the late nineteenth century until the 1970s, largely due to the introduction of new cultigens and seeds and boosted by the availability of fertile land. Since the 1970s, African economies have not benefited from the kinds of productivity increases that Latin America and Asia have experienced and that were associated with the 'green revolution', mainly because the seeds and extensive cultivation techniques of that revolution were inappropriate in the region. When land is relatively abundant and labor is relatively scarce, technologies that involve investment in land, particularly in the form of the capitalization of labor, have much smaller payoffs than they do in, for instance, South Asia.

However, future changes in factor ratios will open up new investment opportunities in Africa. The absolute gaps in investment in human capital in Africa vis-à-vis the rest of the world are smaller in 2010 than they were in 1960. Moreover, while larger cities and higher population densities are associated with substantial policy challenges, they also create economic opportunities. There is already some evidence that African economies are able to benefit from industries that demand a supply of available and affordable labor. Higher population densities both necessitate and make possible new technologies and production techniques. As an increased demand for land justifies 'green revolution' types of investment in Africa, producers may benefit from more efficient and cheaper means of communication. However, large investments in physical infrastructure are required for future expansion and for the physical transportation of produce.

The case of Africa illustrates what one could call 'technological incongruence' (Abramovitz 1986). The new technologies that have been developed have not always been readily transferable to all regions and countries of the world. Differences in factor endowments, among other things, mean that neither the path the West has taken of adopting technologies that require high capital investment nor the path the East has followed of using technologies that work best in an environment rich in labor has been available to African economies. The literature still insists on assessing the relative growth shortfall in Africa in the context of what we know about how development happened in other regions rather than understanding the different conditions in African economies that have been compatible with economic growth. There is much more to learn from country-level success than a story of across-the-board failure.

Since the success of some Asian economies, it has been increasingly fashionable to distill lessons from Asia (or even from Latin America[1]). Learning from how Asian economies succeeded may teach us exactly the opposite – that learning lessons from another development experience may be fraught with misunderstandings. Sugihara has argued that the development paths taken by the 'East' and the 'West' were radically different, and that typically the latter was capital-intensive while the former was labor-intensive (Sugihara 2003). Earlier, Francesca Bray reasoned along similar lines but with a different emphasis. In *The Rice Economies* (1986), she argues that technological development in rice-growing economies was typically land- and labor-intensive, rather than land-extensive and capital-intensive. Rice-growing areas could hold larger population densities, and, while tractors were suitable capital inputs in wheat fields, they were not appropriate for rice fields. In response to Sugihara's formulation of a particular Asian path of development, Gareth Austin suggested that the African precolonial and colonial economies followed quite a different path. In sub-Saharan Africa, labor and capital were scarce, whereas land was relatively abundant. This meant that the typical technique for agricultural production was land-extensive and labor-saving. By extension, it is unlikely that we will see a Meiji Restoration or a Glorious Revolution in sub-Saharan Africa any time soon. The key to understanding what fails or succeeds lies within the economy in question.

Getting African economies right

The solution is to refocus the study of economics on the study of economies. The increasing distance between the observers and the observed has created a growing knowledge problem. With the move to cross-country studies based on macro-analysis, country-level nuances have been lost. In other words, cross-country growth regressions can take us only so far. One of the problems is that the seemingly proven results of such literature have been taken at face value.

The tendency of economics to make law-like statements about the relationship between investment and systems of property rights may be worthwhile for its own sake,[2] but, as Rodrik and others argue, for economics to be relevant to economies, development economists should stop acting as advocates for very specific models of economic development (Rodrik 2010). This is particularly true for the study of African economies. As Gareth Austin (2007) has pointed out, because most models of economic development are derived from studies of Europe and the West, the toolbox of economists is conceptually Eurocentric.

I do not want to argue that economists should be excluded from analyzing the history of political and social institutions. The economic implications of history are far too great for these factors to be sidelined when writing both the history of poverty and the wealth of nations. I do, however, wish to caution economists about the dangers of drawing policy implications for continents – or even for the entire world – that are too quickly based on weak and unquestioned evidence, spurious correlations, and uninvestigated historical relationships.

For both economists and laypeople, it can be hard to keep track of where a carefully specified model ends and where the supporting narrative begins (Morgan 1997; McCloskey 1998). The 'anecdotal' evidence that economists dismiss so readily actually forms the fundamental building blocks needed for the empirical testing of the evidence. In the case of ethnicity, for instance, we are asked to rely on the intuition that ethnicity has been important, and to ignore the fact that the historical experience relating to ethnicity is not consistent with the evidence.

Mainstream economics has a proven superiority in terms of providing influential 'numbers, patterns and stories' to the development community (Jerven 2013c: 431). Recently, economists have begun writing well-digested and masterfully presented narratives for a popular audience based on papers previously published for a scholarly readership. These kinds of books tend to sacrifice nuance and subtlety for clarity. I hope this book will encourage non-economists to read economics more critically. It is often taken as a given that published papers in economics have been through a rigorous scientific process and therefore that they are beyond reproach from non-economists. Economics, econometrics and their use in economic history, called cliometrics, are often couched in a language designed to impress. They use objective evidence, testing a hypothesis with scientific methods to write causal history. In effect, it is the use of numbers and patterns that are fitted into models in order to tell stories. I hope I have shown that simply by asking questions – How good are the numbers? What are the assumptions? How convincing is the story? – one can engage critically with mainstream economics.

The bottom line is that there is no 'Bottom Billion'. The evidence shows that the so-called traps are escapable and the so-called curses are not destiny. The growth literature first told African leaders that they are pursuing the wrong type of policies and then that they had the wrong type of geography and the wrong set of institutions. The turn toward a literature that delivers useful policy recommendations will involve research that seeks to uncover how African states and economies operate, rather than showing how they differ from those that are richer. Karl Marx wrote that the more developed countries showed the less developed the image of their own future. That interpretation of economic development has been debunked time and again.[3] Late development is different, and African countries should follow their own path. If it is true – and I think it is – that institutions really matter for development, then that means we have to understand how and why institutions are embedded, and how we can work with them. The subtraction approach to economic development must be disbanded. A change is needed in the literature on institutions and economic growth – toward a reciprocal comparison focusing on how African economies work rather than only explaining why they don't.

Notes

Introduction

1 26 May 2000, quoted in Bald (2000).

2 Bob Dylan, 'Subterranean homesick blues', single release, Columbia Recording Studios, 1965.

3 For a full list of countries, see Collier (2009).

4 When Easterly and Levine made this comparison, they concluded that ethnic fragmentation explains all the differences between the two countries. Their conclusion, derived from a cross-country growth regression, is that the entire growth difference between Japan (high growth) and Tanzania (low growth) is explained by the difference in ethnic fragmentation and by the fact that Japan is ethnically homogeneous, whereas Tanzania is not. In this comparison, Easterly and Levine relied completely on the variables in their dataset. Their conclusion runs counter to all comparative work on Tanzania and the role of ethnicity and linguistics in its development (Easterly and Levine 1997: 1237).

5 A notable exception is Easterly (2013).

6 *Accelerated Development in Sub-Saharan Africa* (World Bank 1981) is commonly referred to as the Berg report after American economist Elliot Berg, coordinator of the World Bank's African Strategy Review Group.

7 The term 'Washington Consensus' was coined in 1989 by John Williamson, an economist at the Institute for International Economics.

Williamson identified ten policies Washington-based financial institutions such as the IMF and the World Bank adopted as essential prerequisites for financial aid. This became the standard practice in the 1980s; to receive much-needed international financial aid, countries needed to adopt economic reforms that caused serious hardships. These included, among other things, avoiding large deficits relative to GDP, redirecting public spending to service debt, instituting tax reform to broaden the tax base, liberalizing trade, privatizing state-owned enterprises, and deregulating markets.

8 Although the competition is fierce: see Keen (2012), McGovern (2011) and Lawrence (2010).

9 See David Giles, 'Cookbook econometrics', 5 May 2011: http://davegiles.blogspot.ca/2011/05/cookbook-econometrics.html.

10 See Fourcade et al. (2015).

1 Misunderstanding growth in Africa

1 See Helpman (2004) for a good overview of how growth literature has developed.

2 There are a number of papers on this intriguing statistical puzzle (see Matthews 2000).

3 See Mauro (1995) for the seminal paper on this topic.

4 I happened to be in Malawi on field research in the fall of 2010.

5 And, using the previous example, the survey results would

not be influenced in the same way if the survey were conducted in Sweden during a labor dispute between transport workers and their employers.

6 The proxy may seem to be a smart shortcut within economics departments, but I have been told by a colleague that when this paper was first circulated among a group of graduate students in an Indian university, they were certain it was a spoof.

7 Another clever way of saying this is that we treasure what we can measure.

8 Indeed, sometimes country data are made up before the countries exist. See, for instance, the controversy over settler mortality data in the debate between Albouy and Acemoglu, Johnson and Robinson (Acemoglu et al. 2001; Albouy 2012).

9 Wheeler (1984) could be considered an early forerunner in this debate.

10 The first versions of the Penn World Tables were published in the 1970s (Kravis et al. 1978), but the mainstream use of this dataset dates back to the 5.0 version, which was published in 1991 (Summers and Heston 1991).

11 Converting data into logs has many useful properties, and it is often done by economists to make a data series more readily interpretable. In this case, I have converted the data into logs because the range of the data is so large that, if it were plotted on a 'normal' linear scale, you could not see the variation.

12 Note that the World Bank lists 214 countries and territories in its database, but, tellingly, data are missing for GDP per capita and/or per capita growth for 114 countries.

For the 214 countries listed between 1960 and 1990, the World Development Indicators (WDI) database contains only 3,880 observations (out of a possible 6,420 country–year observations, which is 214 countries multiplied by 30 years). I calculated the average rates taken from the observations that are available. Thus, the following countries are excluded from this figure: Afghanistan, Albania, American Samoa, Andorra, Angola, Antigua and Barbuda, Argentina, Armenia, Aruba, Azerbaijan, Bahrain, Belarus, Bhutan, Bosnia and Herzegovina, Brunei, Bulgaria, Cabo Verde, Cambodia, Cayman Islands, Channel Islands, Comoros, Croatia, Cuba, Curacao, Cyprus, the Czech Republic, Djibouti, Dominica, El Salvador, Equatorial Guinea, Eritrea, Estonia, Ethiopia, the Faroe Islands, French Polynesia, Gambia, the Gaza Strip, Georgia, Germany, Greenland, Grenada, Guam, Guinea, Guinea-Bissau, Haiti, Hungary, Indonesia, Iran, Iraq, Ireland, the Isle of Man, Jordan, Kazakhstan, Kenya, Kiribati, Korea, Kosovo, Kuwait, Kyrgyz Republic, Laos, Latvia, Lebanon, Libya, Liechtenstein, Lithuania, Macao (China), Macedonia, Maldives, Mali, Malta, the Marshall Islands, Mauritius, Micronesia, Moldova, Monaco, Mongolia, Montenegro, Mozambique, Myanmar, Namibia, New Caledonia, the Northern Mariana Islands, Palau, Paraguay, Poland, Qatar, Romania, Russia, Saint Lucia, Saint Martin, Samoa, San Marino, Sao Tome and Principe, Saudi Arabia, Serbia, Sint Maarten, the Slovak Republic, Slovenia, the Solomon Islands, South Sudan, Tajikistan, Tanzania, Timor-Leste (East Timor), Tonga, Tunisia, Turkmenistan, the Turks and Caicos

Islands, Tuvalu, Ukraine, the United Arab Emirates, Uzbekistan, Vanuatu, Vietnam, the West Bank, and Yemen.

13 Jane Guyer (2004) describes this as 'bewilderment': 'when analytical assumptions based on foundational invariance, and proceeding by holding variables constant, became increasingly implausible'.

14 As will be shown here, the initial papers highlighted policy mistakes, while in the latter years institutions were foregrounded. The move from the Washington Consensus to the Post-Washington Consensus was a parallel development. For an exploration of this link, see Stein (2008: 76–84).

15 And I pursued a similar line of argument in a chapter of my thesis that was later revised and published as a review article (Jerven 2011c).

16 In this book, 'Africa' is used as shorthand for sub-Saharan Africa.

17 For a short description of the Maddison data project, see Maddison Project (n.d.).

18 All data are taken from WDI. This conclusion is not an artifact of my use of the WDI data: Ndulu and O'Connell (1999) found the same pattern using Penn World Tables, and Maddison (1995) supports the same conclusion. Nor is this finding an artifact of aggregation; it is supported by individual country experiences, as is shown by Arrighi (2002), using data assembled by Berthélemy and Söderling (2001).

19 'Steady-state growth' is the term the economic literature uses instead of average growth to signify that annual changes are distractions and it is the long-term average that matters.

20 The synthesis article was published in 1999, and one could object that the study is fairly dated. However, as indicated in the previous section, there have not been major significant new findings in the literature since then. This contention is supported by Durlauf et al. (2005), who refer to Collier and Gunning (1999a) and Easterly and Levine (1997) as the authoritative examinations of African growth. An additional review of the regression literature on African growth (Azam et al. 2002) focused on the same articles I review here.

21 Easterly and Roodman (2004) reran their work and found that aid does not work.

22 See Jerven (2014a), which uses data from the WDIs (World Bank 2002) and finds a correlation coefficient of -0.985 between GDP growth and literacy rates for the period 1970–2000 (annual data for sub-Saharan Africa).

23 Bleaney and Nishiyama (2002) found this after synthesizing the regression models of Barro (1997), Sachs and Warner (1997) and Easterly and Levine (1997). Their human capital variable is a composite of life expectancy and male schooling.

24 It has also been argued that the problem with African education has been its poor quality and that there has been an overemphasis on tertiary education (Schultz 1999).

25 First *Pick's Currency Yearbook* (New York NY: Pick's Currency Report, various years) and then *World Currency Yearbook* (Brooklyn NY: International Currency Analysis, Inc., various years).

26 For a critique, see Leys (1996).

2 Trapped in history?

1 For a critique of this logic and a review of different growth patterns, see Pritchett (1998).

2 For the year 2000, there were data for 45 countries in sub-Saharan Africa. In these three tests, I looked at agreements and disagreements across the three datasets regarding the relative ranking of countries by GDP per capita (see Jerven 2010d; 2013b). I used data on GDP per capita (in constant 1995 US dollars) from the WDI. The best equivalent from the Penn World Tables is real GDP per capita (the Laspeyres index) in 1996 international Geary dollars. I also used per capita GDP in 1990 international Geary–Khamis dollars from Maddison. Because I was looking at sub-Saharan Africa, I excluded Algeria, Egypt, Libya, Morocco and Tunisia. In addition, the WDI dataset does not have data for Djibouti, Mayotte, Réunion or Somalia, and Maddison lacks a separate estimate for Eritrea (his estimate for Eritrea and Ethiopia is considered to represent Ethiopia).

3 These categories are measures of relative income in the African sample alone and do not match the UN classifications of low-, middle- and high-income economies.

4 In order to establish beyond doubt which group a country belongs to, I used exclusion criteria. I eliminated countries that did not fall within the same cohort according to all three sources on the assumption that the estimates of income for those countries are too inaccurate.

5 I excluded the DRC from this table because its income estimate is undoubtedly too low.

6 As mentioned, some stability exists among the richer countries: Congo-Brazzaville, Côte d'Ivoire, Gabon, Seychelles and South Africa remain among the ten richest throughout the period. The results

of the accuracy exercise I conducted (see Table 2.1) established that only the WDI database places Congo-Brazzaville and Côte d'Ivoire among the ten richest countries. Since there was so much disagreement in the three datasets about these two countries, I excluded them here.

7 Platteau (2009: 676) argues that the fundamental problem in postcolonial Africa has been the 'fluid political setup dominated by unregulated factional competition as well as by the instability of ruling coalitions'.

8 The virtues of 'reciprocal comparison' are well laid out in Pomeranz (2000) and Austin (2007). For a version of the argument relating to endowments and the choice of technology with regard to rice production in Asia, see Bray (1986).

9 They provide no sources for these data.

10 Thanks to Deirdre McCloskey for a reminder of this joke in her excellent review of Boldizzoni's book (McCloskey 2013).

11 The exclusion restriction in their instrumental variable regression is that the mortality rates of European settlers more than 100 years ago have no effect on GDP per capita today, other than their effect through institutional development.

12 For a review and general critique of the use of instrumental variables, see Deaton (2010).

13 For a good perspective on instrumental variables, and why it is not easy to interpret them in a policy context, see Dunning (2011).

14 Taking 'Y' – the income level today – as the starting point is in essence 'doing history backwards', while if one chooses the legacy 'X', there is a risk of 'epochal fallacy'.

Acemoglu and Robinson (2010) arguably provided a perfect example of 'story plucking' when they addressed the issue of why Africa is poor. They picked historical examples from different times and places that supported their general claim without engaging fully with the historical context from which those examples were taken.

15 Manning (2010) has recently argued that the precolonial populations may have been twice as large as indicated in most datasets. Note that the main issue here is not the direction of bias but rather the lack of rigor when discussing the evidence. For further debate see Frankema and Jerven (2014).

16 Of course, it should be recognized that cross-disciplinary work may revise what is perceived as the current state of knowledge in a discipline.

17 Either the effect of institutions, 'X' (as in Bezemer et al. 2009), or as an outcome, 'Y' (as in Fenske 2009; 2010b; 2011).

18 In email correspondence regarding the 'Human Relations Area Files', London School of Economics and Political Science (LSE) anthropology professor Chris Fuller described them as 'a blast from the past' and noted that, apart from Jack Goody, anthropologists in the UK did not rate the files highly. Tobin (1990: 478) summarizes the criticisms of the database made in the 1960s and 1970s and notes that 'critiques have grown rarer recently, not, I think, because the heirs to Boas, Benedict, Leach, and Geertz have grown less antagonistic to quantification and comparison, but because, if they think of HRAF at all, they tend to think of it as moribund'.

19 Similar concerns apply to the use of the dated and crude proxies for 'social capital' (as in the Adelman and Morris dataset in Temple and Johnson 1998) and 'ethnic fractionalization' (as with the index computed from *Atlas Narodov Mira* in Easterly and Levine 1997). Fenske (2010a: 183) notes that the latter dataset has been coded by Posner (2004) to capture 'politically relevant groups'. That may raise more problems than it solves when considering it as historical evidence.

20 For further case studies of the issues arising from problems with the quality of data in economic growth analysis, see Jerven (2010a on Botswana; 2011d on Kenya; 2011b on Tanzania). For an attempt to historicize the African national income data, see Jerven (2011e).

21 Matt Andrews (2014) suggests that the reason why institutional reform fails is closely linked to this misunderstanding. Countries subscribe to an institutional reform that is not real, but just signals an aspiration to follow the accepted rules.

3 African growth recurring

1 For those unfamiliar with the historiography of slavery, this might seem a controversial point. At face value it is indeed a bit of a puzzle that areas that were relatively labor scarce specialized in exporting labor in the form of slaves. The clearest exposition of the puzzle and a suggestion to its solution is provided by Fenoaltea (1999), and more references and a coherent summary are provided by Austin (2009a).

2 Szereszewski assumes that the traditional sector grows at the rate of the population in relative stagnation.

3 Using similar data and methods,

Moradi (2009) found the same in Kenya.

4 These data were retrieved from data collected from army recruits in World War One and World War Two, so they pertain only to men. We do not know what the growth trajectories were for the women in these two cohorts.

5 However, Austin (1996: 559) highlights the importance of small trucks from the 1920s onward.

6 This is further summarized in Jerven (2014b).

7 To some extent, the findings are shaped by the fact that I used the Maddison dataset rather than data from the WDI, the African Development Bank, or the Penn World Tables. Ideally, one should use the primary source – the official national account files – but those have not yet been collected systematically. My study of the quality of the postcolonial growth evidence found that most of the errors in the data are eliminated if one averages growth over periods longer than five years and that there were fewer erroneous growth fluctuations in the Maddison dataset than in the Penn World Tables and the WDI (Jerven 2010b).

8 The nine-year moving average is obtained by calculating the average of nine annual observations taken from the middle-year observation and from four years on each side. Of course, when nine-year moving averages are calculated, the dataset covers only 1955 to 2002.

9 A full list of countries and the observations of sustained growth by country is given in Jerven (2010b).

10 See, for instance, Drummond et al. (2014).

4 Africa's statistical tragedy?

1 In fact, the median is identical. The median is 2001 in the IMF table as well.

2 According to information provided to me from the statistical office of Burundi, that nation has a base year of 2006, not 1996, as reported in Table 4.1. Furthermore, according to information provided to me from the United Nations Economic Commission for Africa, Madagascar has a base year of 1995, and the statistical office is currently preparing to implement the UN's System of National Accounts 2008 (and presumably undertake a rebasing) for 2016. In *Poor Numbers*, I reported a base year of 1997 for Mali (compared with 1987, as reported in Table 4.1) based on information provided to me from the Mali Statistical Office. The provenance of the information the IMF and African Development Bank provide is not detailed in their reports, whereas in *Poor Numbers* I described how all the data were retrieved in the appendix (Jerven 2013b: 123–37).

3 Sudan is missing from the IMF table, and it was not possible to retrieve information from that country for *Poor Numbers*. The African Development Bank lists it among the countries with a base year that is two decades or more old.

4 Angola is one of the fastest growers; its base year is 1987.

5 For a description of the Demographic and Health Surveys and the data used, see Young (2012: 733–6).

6 A fourth alternative is the use of anthropometrics; see, for instance, Moradi and Baten (2005).

7 Using luminosity data, Henderson, Storeygard and Weil (2012: 1020) find that 'growth is more likely to

be underestimated in the WDI for countries with low measured income growth rates, and overestimated in the WDI for some countries showing very high growth rates. But there is a lot of variation across countries in the adjustment.'

8 Annual data are available dating back to 1992.

9 UN-WIDER is the United Nations University World Institute for Development Economics Research.

10 According to a peer review of the Ghana revision commissioned by the African Development Bank, the informal sector is not included in the new GDP numbers, and growth is entirely driven by the formal sector.

11 See www.ft.com/intl/cms/s/0/da7121ba-8802-11e2-8e3c-00144feabdco.html?siteedition=intl#axzz2fieCV9p3.

12 This story broke in *African Arguments* (see Taylor 2013) and was widely reported in the media (see, for example, York 2013).

13 See www.ft.com/intl/cms/s/0/3bb87da0-3fce-11e3-8882-00144feabdco.html#axzz3Srb4zNnv.

Conclusion

1 For an argument about how some scholars think Latin American history may be replayed with a delay of a century and a half in Africa, see Bates et al. (2007).

2 As the joke goes, the economist is the one who finds something that works in practice, and then wonders whether it works in theory.

3 Starting with Gerschenkron (1962), who posited that late development is different, there have been many good reminders that development takes different shapes. For a review of these, see Jerven (2012b).

Bibliography

Abramovitz, M. (1986) 'Catching up, forging ahead, and falling behind'. *Journal of Economic History* 46(2): 385–406.

Acemoglu, D. and J. Robinson (2010) 'Why is Africa poor?' *Economic History of Developing Regions* 25(1): 21–50.

— (2012) *Why Nations Fail: The origins of power, prosperity, and poverty*. New York NY: Random House/Crown.

Acemoglu, D., S. H. Johnson and J. A. Robinson (2001) 'The colonial origins of comparative development: an empirical investigation'. *American Economic Review* 91(5): 1369–401.

— (2002) 'Reversal of fortune: geography and institutions in the making of the modern world income distribution'. *Quarterly Journal of Economics* 117(4): 1231–94.

— (2003) 'An African success story: Botswana'. In D. Rodrik (ed.) *Search of Prosperity: Analytic narratives on economic growth*. Princeton NJ: Princeton University Press, pp. 80–122.

— (2005) 'A response to Albouy's "A Reexamination Based on Improved Settler Mortality Data"'. Unpublished paper.

— (2011) 'Hither thou shalt come, but no further: reply to "The Colonial Origins of Comparative Development: An Empirical Investigation: Comment"'. NBER Working Paper w16966. Cambridge MA: National Bureau of Economic Research (NBER).

http://papers.ssrn.com/sol3/papers.cfm?abstract_id=1820078##.

African Development Bank (2011) *Africa in 50 Years' Time: The road towards inclusive growth*. Tunis: African Development Bank.

— (2013) *Situational Analysis of Economic Statistics in Africa: Special focus on GDP measurement*. Tunis: African Development Bank. www.afdb.org/fileadmin/uploads/afdb/Documents/Publications/Economic%20Brief%20-%20Situational%20Analysis%20of%20the%20Reliability%20of%20Economic%20Statistics%20in%20Africa-%20Special%20Focus%20on%20GDP%20Measurement.pdf.

Aidt, T. S. (2009) 'Corruptions, institutions and economic development'. Cambridge Working Papers in Economics 0918. Cambridge: University of Cambridge. www.econ.cam.ac.uk/research/repec/cam/pdf/cwpe0918.pdf.

Albouy, D. (2004) 'The colonial origins of comparative development: a reexamination based on improved settler mortality data'. Berkeley CA: University of California. http://eml.berkeley.edu/~webfac/dromer/e237_F04/albouy.pdf.

— (2008) 'The colonial origins of comparative development: an investigation of the settler mortality data'. NBER Working Paper 14130. Cambridge MA: National Bureau of Economic Research (NBER). www.nber.org/papers/w14130.

— (2012) 'The colonial origins of

comparative development: an empirical investigation: comment'. *American Economic Review* 102(6): 3059–76.

Alden, C. (2007) *China in Africa*. London and New York NY: Zed Books.

Andrews, M. (2014) *The Limits of Institutional Reform in Development: Changing rules for realistic solutions*. Cambridge: Cambridge University Press.

Arrighi, G. (2002) 'The African crisis: world systemic and regional aspects'. *New Left Review* 15 (May–June): 5–36.

Artadi, E. V. and X. Sala-i-Martin (2003) 'The economic tragedy of the XXth century: growth in Africa'. NBER Working Paper 9865. Cambridge MA: National Bureau of Economic Research (NBER).

Austin, G. (1996) 'National poverty and the "vampire state" in Ghana: a review article'. *Journal of International Development* 8(4): 553–73.

— (2005) *Labour, Land and Capital in Ghana: From slavery to free labour in Asante, 1807–1956*. Rochester NY: University of Rochester Press.

— (2007) 'Reciprocal comparison and African history: tackling conceptual eurocentrism in the study of Africa's economic past'. *African Studies Review* 50(3): 1–28.

— (2008a) 'Resources, techniques, and strategies south of the Sahara: revising the factor endowments perspective on African economic development, 1500–2000'. *Economic History Review* 61(3): 587–624.

— (2008b) 'The "reversal of fortune" thesis and the compression of history: perspectives from African and comparative economic history'. *Journal of International Development* 20(8): 996–1027.

— (2009a) 'Factor markets in Nieboer conditions: early modern West Africa c.1500–c.1900'. *Continuity and Change* 24 (Special): 23–53.

— (2009b) 'Poverty and development in sub-Saharan Africa, c.1450–c.1900: reflections on the development of the economic historiography'. Paper presented at the annual meeting of the European Historical Economics Society, Geneva, 4 September.

— (2011) *Labour-intensive Industrialization in Global History*. London: Routledge.

— (2012) 'Vent for surplus or productivity breakthrough? The Ghanaian cocoa take-off, c.1890–1936'. Paper presented at the Conference on Trade, Poverty and Growth in History, Madrid, 17–18 May.

Auty, R. M. (2001) *Resource Abundance and Economic Development*. New York NY: Oxford University Press.

Azam, J. P. (2007) *Trade, Exchange Rate, and Growth in Sub-Saharan Africa*. Cambridge: Cambridge University Press.

— A. Fosu and N. S. Ndung'u (2002) 'Explaining slow growth in Africa'. *African Development Review* 14(2): 177–220.

Bald, M. (2000) 'The hopeless continent'. *World Press Review* 47(10). worldpressreview.org/Africa/1306. cfm.

Banerjee, A. and E. Duflo (2011) *Poor Economics: A radical rethinking of the way to fight global poverty*. New York NY: PublicAffairs.

Bardhan, P. (2005) 'Institutions matter, but which ones?' *Economics of Transition* 13: 499–532.

Barro, R. J. (1991) 'Economic growth in a cross section of countries'. *Quarterly Journal of Economics* 106(2): 407–43.

— (1997) *Determinants of Economic Growth: Cross-country empirical study.* Cambridge MA: MIT Press.

Bates, R. H. (1981) *Markets and States in Tropical Africa: The political basis of agricultural policies.* Berkeley CA: University of California Press.

— (1983) *Essays on the Political Economy of Rural Africa.* Cambridge: Cambridge University Press.

— J. H. Coatsworth and J. G. Williamson (2007) 'Lost decades: post-independence performance in Latin America and Africa'. *Journal of Economic History* 67(4): 917–43.

Battacharyya, S. (2009) 'Root causes of African underdevelopment'. *Journal of African Economies* 18(5): 745–80.

Bayart, J.-F. (2000) 'Africa in the world: a history of extraversion'. *African Affairs* 99(395): 217–67.

Bennell, P. (2002) 'Hitting the target: doubling primary school enrollments in sub-Saharan Africa by 2015'. *World Development* 30(7): 1179–94.

Berman, B. (1990) *Control and Crisis in Colonial Kenya: The dialectic of domination.* London, Nairobi and Athens OH: J. Currey, Heinemann Kenya and Ohio University Press.

Berry, S. (2002) 'Debating the land question in Africa'. *Comparative Studies in Society and History* 44(4): 638–68.

Berthélemy, J. C. and L. Söderling (2001) 'The role of capital accumulation, adjustment and structural change for economic take-off: empirical evidence from African growth episodes'. *World Development* 29: 323–43.

Besley, T. and R. Burgess (2000) 'Land reform, poverty reduction, and growth: evidence from India'. *Quarterly Journal of Economics* 115(2): 389–430.

Bezemer, D., J. Bolt and R. Lensink (2009) 'Indigenous slavery in Africa's history: conditions and consequences'. Paper presented at the Centre for the Study of African Economies (CSAE) conference, 22–24 March. www.csae. ox.ac.uk/conferences/2009-EDIA/ papers/095-Lensink.pdf.

Blattman, C. and E. Miguel (2010) 'Civil war'. *Journal of Economic Literature* 48(1): 3–57.

Bleaney, M. and A. Nishiyama (2002) 'Explaining growth: a contest between models'. *Journal of Economic Growth* 7(1): 43–56.

Bloom, D. E. and J. D. Sachs (1998) 'Geography, demography, and economic growth in Africa'. *Brookings Papers on Economic Activity* 1998(2): 207–96.

Bockstette, V., A. Chanda and L. Putterman (2002) 'States and markets: the advantage of an early start'. *Journal of Economic Growth* 7(4): 347–69.

Bowden, S., B. Chiripanhura and P. Mosley (2008) 'Measuring and explaining poverty in six African countries: a long period approach'. *Journal of International Development* 20(8): 1049–79.

Brautigam, D. (2009) *The Dragon's Gift: The real story of China in Africa.* Oxford and New York NY: Oxford University Press.

— O.-H. Fjeldstand and M. Moore (2008) *Taxation and State-Building in Developing Countries: Capacity and consent.* New York NY: Cambridge University Press.

Bray, F. (1986) *The Rice Economies: Technology and development in Asian societies.* Oxford: Basil Blackwell.

Bruk, S. I. and V. S. Apenchenko (eds) (1964) *Atlas narodov mira* [*Atlas of the Peoples of the World*]. Moscow: Glavnoe upravlenie geodezii i kartografii Gosudarstvennogo geologicheskogo komiteta SSSR, Institut etnografii i m. N.N. Miklukho-Maklaia Akademii Nauk SSSR.

Burnside, C. and D. Dollar (2000) 'Aid, policies, and growth'. *American Economic Review* 90(4): 847–68.

Carr-Hill, R. (2013) 'Measuring development progress in Africa: the denominator problem'. Paper presented at the Conference on African Economic Development: Measuring Success and Failure, School for International Studies, Simon Fraser University, Vancouver, 18–20 April.

Chen, X. and W. Nordhaus (2010) 'The value of luminosity data as a proxy for economic statistics'. NBER Working Paper 16317. Cambridge MA: National Bureau of Economic Research (NBER).

Cheru, F. and C. Obi (2010) *The Rise of China and India in Africa: Challenges, opportunities and critical interventions*. London: Zed Books.

Collier, P. (1993) 'Africa and the study of economics'. In R. H. Bates, V. Y. Mudimbe and J. F. O'Barr (eds) *Africa and the Disciplines: The contributions of research in Africa to the social sciences and humanities*. Chicago IL: Chicago University Press, pp. 56–83.

— (2007) *The Bottom Billion: Why the poorest countries are failing and what can be done about it*. New York NY: Oxford University Press.

— (2009) *Wars, Guns, and Votes: Democracy in dangerous places*. New York NY: Harper.

— and J. Gunning (1999a) 'Explaining African economic performance'. *Journal of Economic Literature* 37(1): 64–111.

— (1999b) 'Why has Africa grown slowly?' *Journal of Economic Perspectives* 13(3): 3–22.

Cooper, F. (1993) 'Africa and the world economy'. In F. Cooper, A. Isaacman, F. Mallon, W. Roseberry and S. Stern (eds) *Confronting Historical Paradigms: Peasants, labour and the capitalist world system in African and Latin America*. Madison WI: University of Wisconsin Press, pp. 84–203.

— (2002) *Africa Since 1940: The past of the present*. New York NY: Cambridge University Press.

— (2005) *Colonialism in Question: Theory, knowledge, history*. Berkeley CA: University of California Press.

Crafts, N. (2002) 'The Solow productivity paradox in historical perspective'. CEPR Discussion Paper 3142. London: Centre for Economic Policy Research (CEPR).

Cramer, C. (2006) *Violence in Developing Countries: War, memory, progress*. Bloomington IN: Indiana University Press.

Deaton, A. (1999) 'Commodity prices and growth in Africa'. *Journal of Economic Perspectives* 13(3): 23–40.

— (2010) 'Instruments, randomization, and learning about development'. *Journal of Economic Literature* 48(2): 424–55.

Deverajan, S. (2013) 'Africa's statistical tragedy'. *Review of Income and Wealth* 59 (Supplement 1): S9–S15.

— W. Easterly and H. Pack (2001) 'Is investment in Africa too high or too low? Macro- and micro-evidence'. *Journal of African Economies* 10(2): 81–108.

Diouf, S. A. (2003) 'Introduction'. In S. A. Diouf (ed.) *Fighting the Slave Trade: West African strategies*. Athens OH: Ohio University Press, pp. ix–xxvii.

Dowrick, S. and J. Delong (2003) 'Globalization and convergence'. In M. Bordo, A. Taylor and J. G. Williamson (eds) *Globalization in Historical Perspective*. Chicago IL: University of Chicago Press, pp. 191–220.

Drummond, P., V. Thakoor and S. Yu (2014) 'Africa Rising: Harnessing the demographic dividend'. Working Paper 14/143. Washington DC: International Monetary Fund (IMF). https://www.imf.org/external/pubs/cat/longres.aspx?sk=41819.0.

Dunning, T. (2011) 'Instrumental variables'. In B. Badie, D. Berg-Schlosser and L. Morlino (eds) *International Encyclopedia of Political Science*. London: Sage Publications.

Durlauf, S., P. Johnson and J. Temple (2005) 'Growth econometrics'. In P. Aghion and S. Durlauf (eds) *Handbook of Economic Growth*. Amsterdam: Elsevier, pp. 555–667.

Easterly, W. (2001a) *The Elusive Quest for Growth: Economists' adventures and misadventures in the tropics*. Cambridge MA: Cambridge University Press.

— (2001b) 'Global development network growth database'. Washington DC: World Bank. http://econ.worldbank.org/WBSITE/EXTERNAL/EXTDEC/EXTRESEARCH/0,,contentMDK:20701055~pagePK:64214825~piPK:64214943~theSitePK:469382,00.html.

— (2001c) 'The lost decades: explaining developing countries' stagnation in spite of policy reform, 1980–1998'. *Journal of Economic Growth* 6(2): 135–57.

— (2006) *The White Man's Burden: Why the West's efforts to aid the rest have done so much ill and so little good*. New York NY: Penguin Press.

— (2009) 'The burden of proof should be on interventionists – doubt is a superb reason for inaction'. *Boston Review*, July/August. http://new.bostonreview.net/BR34.4/easterly.php.

— (2013) *The Tyranny of Experts: Economists, dictators, and the forgotten rights of the poor*. New York NY: Basic Books.

— and R. Levine (1997) 'Africa's growth tragedy: policies and ethnic divisions'. *Quarterly Journal of Economics* 112(4): 1203–50.

— and D. Roodman (2004) 'New data, new doubts: a comment on Burnside and Dollar's "Aid, Policies, and Growth" (2000)'. *American Economic Review* 94(3): 774–80.

— M. Kremer, L. Pritchett and L. H. Summers (1993) 'Good policy or good luck? Country growth performance and temporary shocks'. *Journal of Monetary Economics* 32: 459–83.

Economist (2000) 'The heart of the matter'. *The Economist*, 11 May. www.economist.com/node/333437.

— (2011) 'The hopeful continent: Africa rising'. *The Economist*, 3 December. www.economist.com/node/21541015.

— (2014) 'Nigeria: Africa's new number one'. *The Economist*, 12 April. www.economist.com/news/leaders/21600685-nigerias-suddenly-supersized-economy-indeed-wonder-so-are-its-still-huge.

Englebert, P. (2000a) 'Pre-colonial

institutions, post-colonial states, and economic development in tropical Africa'. *Political Research Quarterly* 53(1): 7–36.

— (2000b) 'Solving the mystery of the African dummy'. *World Development* 28(10): 1821–35.

Etzo, S. and G. Collender (2010) 'The mobile phone "revolution" in Africa: rhetoric or reality?' *African Affairs* 109(437): 659–68.

Fearon, J. and D. Laitin (2003) 'Ethnicity, insurgency, and civil war'. *American Political Science Review* 97(1): 75–90.

Fenoaltea, S. (1999) 'Europe in the African mirror: the slave trade and the rise of feudalism'. *Rivista di storia economica* 2 (August): 123–66.

Fenske, J. (2009) 'Does land abundance explain African institutions?' Working Paper 981. New Haven CT: Economic Growth Center, Yale University.

— (2010a) 'The causal history of Africa: a response to Hopkins'. *Economic History of Developing Regions* 25(2): 177–212.

— (2010b) 'Ecology, trade and states in pre-colonial Africa'. www.econ. upf.edu/docs/seminars/fenske.pdf.

— (2011a) 'African polygamy: past and present'. www.lse.ac.uk/ economichistory/seminars/ modernandcomparative/papers 2011-12/fenske.pdf.

— (2011b) 'The causal history of Africa: replies to Jerven and Hopkins'. *Economic History of Developing Regions* 2: 125–31.

Ferguson, J. (2007) *Global Shadows: Africa in the neoliberal world order.* Durham NC: Duke University Press.

Fisman, R. and E. Miguel (2008) *Economic Gangsters: Corruption, violence, and the poverty of nations.* Princeton NJ: Princeton University Press.

Flint, J. E. and E. A. McDougall (1987) 'Economic change in West Africa in the nineteenth century'. In J. F. A. Ajayi and M. Crowder (eds) *History of West Africa: Volume 2.* Harlow: Longman.

Fourcade, M., E. Ollion and Y. Algan (2015) 'The superiority of economists'. *Journal of Economic Perspectives* 29(1): 89–114.

Frankema, E. and M. Jerven (2014) 'Writing history backwards or sideways: towards a consensus on African population, 1850–present'. *Economic History Review* 67(4): 907–31.

Frankema, E. and M. van Waijenburg (2012) 'Structural impediments to African growth? New evidence from real wages in British Africa, 1880–1940'. *Journal of Economic History* 73(4): 895–926.

Gerschenkron, A. (1962) *Economic Backwardness in Historical Perspective: A book of essays.* Cambridge MA: Belknap Press, Harvard University Press.

Go, D. S. and J. Page (2008) *Africa at a Turning Point?* Washington DC: World Bank.

Guinnane, T. W., W. A. Sundstrom and W. Whatley (eds) (2004) *History Matters: Essays on economic growth, technology, and demographic change.* Stanford CA: Stanford University Press.

Guyer, J. I. (2004) *Marginal Gains: Monetary transactions in Atlantic Africa.* Chicago IL: University of Chicago Press.

Harriss, J. (2002) 'The case for cross-disciplinary approaches in international development'. *World Development* 30: 487–96.

Harttgen, K., S. Klasen and S. Vollmer (2013) 'An African growth miracle? Or: what do asset indices tell us about trends in economic performance?' *Review of Income and Wealth* 59 (Supplement S1): S37–S61.

Helleiner, G. K. (1966) *Peasant Agriculture, Government, and Economic Growth in Nigeria*. Homewood IL: R. D. Irwin.

Helpman, E. (2004) *The Mystery of Economic Growth*. Cambridge MA: Harvard University Press.

Henderson, J. V., A. Storeygard and D. N. Weil (2012) 'Measuring growth from outer space'. *American Economic Review* 102(2): 994–1028.

Herbst, J. (2000) *States and Power in Africa: Comparative lessons in authority and control*. Princeton NJ: Princeton University Press.

Heston, A. (1994) 'A brief review of some problems in using national accounts data in level of output comparisons and growth studies'. *Journal of Development Economics* 44(1): 29–52.

— R. Summers and B. Aten (2006) *Penn World Table Version 6.2*. Philadelphia PA: Center for International Comparisons of Production, Income and Prices, University of Pennsylvania.

Hill, P. (1970) *Studies in Rural Capitalism in West Africa*. Cambridge: Cambridge University Press.

Hopkins, A. G. (1973) *An Economic History of West Africa*. London: Longman.

— (1986) 'The World Bank in Africa: historical reflections on the African present'. *World Development* 14(12): 1473–87.

— (2009) 'The new economic history of Africa'. *Journal of African History* 50(2): 155–77.

— (2011) 'Causes and confusions in African history'. *Economic History of Developing Regions* 2: 107–10.

Hunt, D. and M. Lipton (2011) 'Green revolutions for sub-Saharan Africa?' Briefing paper. London: Chatham House.

IMF (2012a) *Regional Economic Outlook: Sub-Saharan Africa: Weathering the storm*. Washington DC: International Monetary Fund (IMF).

— (2012b) *World Economic Outlook, October 2012: Coping with high debt and sluggish growth*. Washington DC: International Monetary Fund (IMF). www.imf.org/external/pubs/ft/weo/2012/02/.

— (2013) *Regional Economic Outlook: Sub-Saharan Africa: Building momentum in a multi-speed world*. Washington DC: International Monetary Fund (IMF). www.imf.org/external/pubs/ft/reo/2013/afr/eng/sreo0513.pdf.

— (2014) *IMF Forecasts: Process, quality and country perspectives*. Washington DC: International Monetary Fund (IMF).

Inikori, J. E. (2003) 'The struggle against the transatlantic slave trade: the role of the state'. In S. A. Diouf (ed.) *Fighting the Slave Trade: West African strategies*. Athens OH: Ohio University Press, pp. 170–98.

— (2007) 'Africa and the globalization process: western Africa, 1450–1850'. *Journal of Global History* 2(1): 63–86.

Jack, A. (2013) 'Africa counts the cost of miscalculations'. *Financial Times*, 24 February. http://www.ft.com/cms/s/2/0168741a-7c4d-11e2-91d2-00144feabdc0.html#axzz2fieCV9p3.

Jácome, L. I., A. Alichi, I. L. de

Oliveira Lima and J. I. Canales Kriljenko (2010) 'Weathering the global storm: the benefits of monetary policy reform in the LA5 countries'. IMF Working Paper WP/10/292. Washington DC: International Monetary Fund (IMF). www.imf.org/external/pubs/ft/wp/2010/wp10292.pdf.

Jedwab, R. and A. Moradi (2011) 'Transportation infrastructure and development in Ghana'. Working Paper 2011-24. Paris: Paris School of Economics. http://halshs.archives-ouvertes.fr/docs/00/60/72/07/PDF/wp201124.pdf.

Jenkins, R. (2006) 'Where development meets history'. *Commonwealth and Comparative Politics* 44(1): 2–15.

Jerven, M. (2008) 'African economic growth reconsidered: measurement and performance in East-Central Africa, 1965–1995'. PhD dissertation, London School of Economics.

— (2010a) 'Accounting for the African growth miracle: the official evidence, Botswana 1965–1995'. *Journal of Southern African Studies* 36(1): 73–94.

— (2010b) 'African growth recurring: an economic history perspective on African growth episodes, 1690–2010'. *Economic History of Developing Regions* 25(2): 127–54.

— (2010c) 'Random growth in Africa? A report on the quality of the growth evidence in East-Central Africa, 1965–1995'. *Journal of Development Studies* 46(2): 274–94.

— (2010d) 'The relativity of poverty and income: how reliable are African economic statistics?' *African Affairs* 109(434): 77–96.

— (2011a) 'A clash of disciplines? Economists and historians approaching the African past'. *Economic History of Developing Regions* 26(2): 111–24.

— (2011b) 'Growth, stagnation or retrogression? On the accuracy of economic observations, Tanzania, 1961–2001'. *Journal of African Economies* 20(3): 377–94.

— (2011c) 'The quest for the African dummy: explaining African postcolonial economic performance revisited'. *Journal of International Development* 23(2): 288–307.

— (2011d) 'Revisiting the consensus on Kenyan economic growth, 1964–1995'. *Journal of Eastern African Studies* 5(1): 2–23.

— (2011e) 'Users and producers of African income: measuring the progress of African economies'. *African Affairs* 110(439): 169–90. doi: 10.1093/afraf/adq079; http://mortenjerven.com/wp-content/uploads/2013/02/users-and-producers-AA-jerven.pdf.

— (2012a) 'Poor numbers: how we are misled by African development statistics and what to do about it'. African Arguments, 20 November. http://africanarguments.org/2012/11/20/poor-numbers-how-we-are-misled-by-african-development-statistics-and-what-to-do-about-it-%E2%80%93-by-morten-jerven/.

— (2012b) 'An unlevel playing field: national income estimates and reciprocal comparison in global economic history'. *Journal of Global History* 7(1): 107–28.

— (2013a) 'Briefing. For richer, for poorer: GDP revisions and Africa's statistical tragedy'. *African Affairs* 112(146): 138–47.

— (2013b) *Poor Numbers: How we are misled by African development* statistics and what to do about it. Ithaca NY: Cornell University Press.

— (2013c) 'Reading economics: the role of mainstream economics in international development studies today'. *Canadian Journal of Development Studies* 34(3): 431–40.

— (2014a) *Economic Growth and Measurement Reconsidered in Botswana, Kenya, Tanzania, and Zambia, 1965–1995*. New York NY: Oxford University Press.

— (2014b) 'A West African experiment: constructing a GDP series for colonial Ghana, 1891–1950'. *Economic History Review* 67(4): 964–92.

— (2014c) 'What does Nigeria's new GPD number actually mean?' African Arguments, 8 April. http://africanarguments.org/2014/04/08/what-does-nigerias-new-gdp-number-actually-mean-by-morten-jerven/.

— (2014d) 'African growth miracle or statistical tragedy? Interpreting trends in the data over the past two decades'. WIDER Working Paper 2014/114. Helsinki: UNU-WIDER.

— (2014e) 'Measuring African development: past and present'. *Canadian Journal of Development Studies* 35(1): 1–8.

— (2014f) 'On the accuracy of trade and GDP statistics in Africa: errors of commission and omission'. *Journal of African Trade*, forthcoming.

— and M. Ebo Duncan (2012) 'Revising GDP estimates in sub-Saharan Africa: lessons from Ghana'. *African Statistical Journal* 15: 12–24.

— and D. Johnston (2015) 'Statistical tragedy in Africa? Evaluating the data base for African economic development'. *Journal of Development Studies*, forthcoming.

— M. Ebo Duncan, Y. Kale and M. Nyoni (2015) 'GDP revisions and updating statistical systems in sub-Saharan Africa: reports from the statistical offices in Nigeria, Liberia, and Zimbabwe'. *Journal of Development Studies*, forthcoming.

— G. Austin, E. Green, C. Uche, E. Frankema, J. Fourie, J. E. Inikori, A. Moradi and E. Hillbom (2012) 'Moving forward in African economic history: bridging the gap in methods and sources'. Working Paper 1. African Economic History Network. www.aehnetwork.org/wp-content/uploads/2012/05/AEHN-WP-1.pdf.

Johnston, D. and A. Abreu (2013) 'Asset indices as a proxy for poverty measurement in African countries: a reassessment'. Paper presented at the Conference on African Economic Development: Measuring Success and Failure, School for International Studies, Simon Fraser University, Vancouver, 18–20 April.

Jones, E. L. (1988) *Growth Recurring: Economic change in world history*. Oxford and New York NY: Clarendon Press and Oxford University Press.

Kaufmann, D., A. Kraay and P. Zoido-Labatón (1999) 'Governance matters'. World Bank Policy Research Working Paper 2196. Washington DC: World Bank.

Kawa, L. (2012) 'The 20 fastest growing economies in the world'. *Business Insider*, 24 October. www.businessinsider.com/worlds-fastest-economies-2012-10?op=1.

Keen, D. (2012) 'Greed and grievance in civil war'. *International Affairs* 88(4): 757–77.

Kelsall, T. (2013) *Business, Politics, and the State in Africa: Challenging the orthodoxies on growth and transformation*. London: Zed Books.

Kenny, C. (2005) 'Why are we worried about income?' *World Development* 33(1): 1–19.

— and D. Williams (2001) 'What do we know about economic growth? Or, why don't we know very much?' *World Development* 29(1): 1–21.

Kiregyera, B. (2013) 'The dawning of a statistical renaissance in Africa'. Paper presented at the Conference on African Economic Development: Measuring Success and Failure, School for International Studies, Simon Fraser University, Vancouver, 18–20 April.

Klein, M. A. (2001) 'The slave trade and decentralized societies'. *Journal of African History* 42(1): 49–65.

Knack, S. and P. Keefer (1995) 'Institutions and economic performance: cross-country tests using alternative measures'. *Economics and Politics* 7(3): 207–27.

Kravis, I. B., A. W. Heston and R. Summers (1978) 'Real GDP per capita for more than one hundred countries'. *Economic Journal* 88(350): 215–42.

Law, R. (1995) *From Slave Trade to 'Legitimate' Commerce: The commercial transition in nineteenth-century West Africa*. Cambridge and New York NY: Cambridge University Press.

Lawrence, P. (2010) 'Development by numbers'. *New Left Review* 62 (March-April). http://newleft review.org/II/62/peter-lawrence-development-by-numbers.

Ley, E. and F. Misch (2014) 'Output revisions in low income countries'. Paper presented at the joint RES-SPR Conference on Macroeconomic Challenges Facing Low-Income Countries, hosted by the International Monetary Fund with support from the UK Department for International Development (DfID), Washington, DC, 30–31 January 2014.

Leys, C. (1996) *The Rise and Fall of Development Theory*. Nairobi and Bloomington IN: EAEP and Indiana University Press.

Lipton, M. (2012) 'Income from work: the food-population-resource crisis in the "short Africa"'. Leontief Prize Lecture, Tufts University, 3 April. www.ase.tufts.edu/gdae/about_us/leontief/LiptonLeontief PrizeComments.pdf.

Lovejoy, P. E. and J. S. Hogendorn (1993) *Slow Death for Slavery: The course of abolition in northern Nigeria, 1837–1936*. Cambridge and New York NY: Cambridge University Press.

Lucas, R. E. (1990) 'Why doesn't capital flow from rich to poor countries?' *American Economic Review* 80(2): 92–7.

Maddison, A. (1995) *Monitoring the World Economy, 1820–1992*. Paris: OECD.

— (2003) *The World Economy: Historical statistics*. Paris: OECD.

— (2009) 'Historical statistics of the world economy: 1–2006 AD'. Groningen: Maddison Project, University of Groningen. www.ggdc.net/maddison/.

Maddison Project (n.d.) 'Maddison Project'. Groningen: Maddison Project, University of Groningen. www.ggdc.net/maddison/.

Mamdani, M. (2001) *When Victims Become Killers: Colonialism, nativism, and the genocide in Rwanda*. Princeton NJ: Princeton University Press.

Manning, P. (1982) *Slavery, Colonialism and Economic Growth in Dahomey, 1640–1960*. Cambridge and New York NY: Cambridge University Press.

— (1987) 'The prospects for African economic history: is today included in the long run?' *African Studies Review* 30(2): 49–62.

— (2010) 'African population: projections 1850–1960'. In K. Ittmann, D. D. Cordell and G. Maddox (eds) *The Demographics of Empire: The colonial order and the creation of knowledge*. Athens OH: Ohio University Press, pp. 245–75.

Maslin, M. (2004) *Global Warming: A very short introduction*. New York NY: Oxford University Press.

Matthews, R. (2000) 'Storks deliver babies (p = 0.008)'. *Teaching Statistics* 22(2): 36–8.

Mauro, P. (1995) 'Corruption and growth'. *Quarterly Journal of Economics* 110(3): 681–712.

McCloskey, D. N. (1998) *The Rhetoric of Economics*. Madison WI: University of Wisconsin Press.

— (2013) 'The poverty of Boldizzoni: resurrecting the German historical school'. *Economic History Research* 9(1). doi: 10.1016/j.ihe.2012.12.002.

McEvedy, C. and R. Jones (1978) *Atlas of World Population History*. Harmondsworth: Penguin Books.

McGovern, M. (2011) 'Popular development economics: an anthropologist among the Mandarins'. *Perspectives on Politics* 9(2): 345–55.

McKay, A. (2013) 'Growth and poverty reduction in Africa in the last two decades: evidence from an AERC growth-poverty project and beyond'. *Journal of African Economies* 22(1): 49–76.

Miguel, E. (2009) *Africa's Turn?* Cambridge MA: MIT Press.

— and C. Blattman (2009) 'Civil war'. NBER Working Paper 14801. Cambridge MA: National Bureau of Economic Research (NBER).

— S. Satyanath and E. Sergenti (2004) 'Economic shocks and civil conflict: an instrumental variables approach'. *Journal of Political Economy* 112(4): 725–53.

Milanovic, B. (2014) 'My take on the Acemoglu–Robinson critique of Piketty'. Globalinequality blog, 23 August. http://glineq.blogspot.fr/2014/08/my-take-on-acemoglu-robinson-critique.html.

Mkandawire, T. (2001) 'Thinking about developmental states in Africa'. *Cambridge Journal of Economics* 25(3): 289–314.

— (2011) 'Running while others walk: knowledge and the challenge of Africa's development'. *Africa Development* 36(2): 1–36.

— and C. C. Soludo (1999) *Our Continent, Our Future: African perspectives on structural adjustment*. Dakar: CODESRIA.

Moradi, A. (2008) 'Confronting colonial legacies: lessons from human development in Ghana and Kenya, 1880–2000'. *Journal of International Development* 20(8): 1107–21.

— (2009) 'Towards an objective account of nutrition and health in colonial Kenya: a study of stature in African army recruits and civilians, 1880–1980'. *Journal of Economic History* 69(3): 719–54.

— and J. Baten (2005) 'Inequality in sub-Saharan Africa: new data and new insights from anthropometric estimates'. *World Development* 33(8): 1233–65.

— G. Austin and J. Baten (2013) 'Heights and development in a cash-crop colony: living standards in Ghana, 1870–1980'. Working Paper Series 7/2013. African Economic History Network. http://www.aehnetwork.org/wp-content/uploads/2012/05/AEHN-WP-7.pdf.

Morgan, M. S. (1997) 'Models, stories, and the economic world'. *Journal of Economic Methodology* 8(3): 361–84.

— (2012) *The World in the Model: How economists work and think.* New York NY: Cambridge University Press.

Mwase, N. and B. J. Ndulu (2008) 'Tanzania: explaining four decades of episodic growth'. In B. J. Ndulu, S. A. O'Connell, J. P. Azam, R. H. Bates, A. K. Fosu, J. W. Gunning and D. Njinkeu (eds) *The Political Economy of Economic of Growth in Africa, 1960–2000: Case studies.* Cambridge: Cambridge University Press, pp. 426–71.

Myint, H. (1958) 'The "classical" theory of international trade and the underdeveloped countries'. *Economic Journal* 68(270): 317–37.

Ncube, M. and A. Shimeles (2013) 'The making of middle class in Africa: evidence from DHS data'. Paper presented at the Conference on African Economic Development: Measuring Success and Failure, School for International Studies, Simon Fraser University, Vancouver, 18–20 April.

Ndulu, B. J. and S. A. O'Connell (1999) 'Governance and growth in sub-Saharan Africa'. *Journal of Economic Perspectives* 13(3): 41–66.

— J. P. Azam, R. H. Bates, A. K. Fosu, J. W. Gunning and D. Njinkeu (2008a) *The Political Economy of Economic of Growth in Africa, 1960–2000. Volume 1: An analytic survey.* Cambridge: Cambridge University Press.

— (2008b) *The Political Economy of Economic of Growth in Africa, 1960–2000. Volume 2: Country case studies.* Cambridge: Cambridge University Press.

North, D. (1990) *Institutions, Institutional Change, and Economic Performance.* Cambridge and New York NY: Cambridge University Press.

Northrup, D. (2002) *Africa's Discovery of Europe, 1450–1850.* New York NY: Oxford University Press.

Nunn, N. (2007) 'Historical legacies: a model linking Africa's past to its current development'. *Journal of Development Economics* 83(1): 157–75.

— (2008) 'The long-term effects of Africa's slave trades'. *Quarterly Journal of Economics* 123(1): 139–76.

— (2009) 'The importance of history for economic development'. NBER Working Paper 14899. Cambridge MA: National Bureau of Economic Research (NBER).

Parker, J. and R. Rathbone (2007) *African History: A very short introduction.* Oxford: Oxford University Press.

Platteau, J.-P. (2009) 'Institutional obstacles to African economic development: state, ethnicity, and custom'. *Journal of Economic Behaviour and Organization* 71(3): 669–89.

Pomeranz, K. (2000) *The Great Divergence: China, Europe, and the making of the modern world economy.* Princeton NJ: Princeton University Press.

Posner, D. N. (2004) 'Measuring ethnic fractionalization in Africa'. *American Journal of Political Science* 48(4): 849–63.

Pritchett, L. (1998) 'Patterns of economic growth: hills, plateaus,

Bibliography

mountains, and plains'. Policy Research Working Paper 1947. Washington DC: World Bank.

— (2001) 'Where has all the education gone?' *World Bank Economic Review* 15(3): 367–91.

— and E. Werker (2012) *Developing the Guts of a GUT (Grand Unified Theory): Elite commitment and inclusive growth*. Manchester: Effective States and Inclusive Development Research Centre (ESID), University of Manchester.

Ray, D. (2010) 'Uneven growth: a framework for research in development economics'. *Journal of Economic Perspectives* 24(3): 45–60.

Reder, M. W. (2003) 'The tension between strong history and strong economics'. In T. W. Guinnane, W. A. Sundstrom and W. Whatley (eds) *History Matters: Essays on economic growth, technology, and demographic change*. Stanford CA: Stanford University Press, pp. 96–113.

Rodney, W. (1972) *How Europe Underdeveloped Africa*. London: Bogle-L'Ouverture Publications.

Rodrik, D. (1998) 'Why do more open economies have bigger governments?' *Journal of Political Economy* 106(5): 997–1032.

— (2010) 'Diagnostics before prescription'. *Journal of Economic Perspectives* 24(3): 33–44.

— A. Subramanian and F. Trebbi (2002) 'Institutions rule: the primacy of institutions over geography and integration in economic development'. NBER Working Paper 9305. Cambridge MA: National Bureau of Economic Research (NBER). www.nber.org/papers/w9305.

Sachs, J. D. (2003) 'Institutions don't rule: direct effects of geography on per capita income'. NBER Working Paper 9490. Cambridge MA: National Bureau of Economic Research (NBER). www.nber.org/papers/w9490.

— (2005) *The End of Poverty: How we can make it happen in our lifetime*. London: Penguin.

— and A. M. Warner (1997) 'Sources of slow growth in African economies'. *Journal of African Economies* 6(3): 335–76.

Sala-i-Martin, X. and M. Pinkovskiy (2010) 'African poverty is falling ... much faster than you think!' NBER Working Paper 15775. Cambridge MA: National Bureau of Economic Research (NBER). www.nber.org/papers/w15775.

Schultz, P. T. (1999) 'Health and schooling investments in Africa'. *Journal of Economic Perspectives* 3(3): 67–88.

Sen, A. K. (1999) *Development as Freedom*. New York NY: Knopf.

Sender, J. (1999) 'Africa's economic performance: limitations of the current consensus'. *Journal of Economic Perspectives* 13(3): 89–114.

Singer, D. J. and M. Small (1994) 'International and civil war data, 1816–1992'. Correlates of War Project, University of Michigan, Department of Political Science.

Smith, S. (1976) 'An extension of the vent-for-surplus model in relation to long-run structural change in Nigeria'. *Oxford Economic Papers* 28(3): 426–46.

Sokoloff, K. and S. Engerman (2000) 'History lessons: institutions, factors endowments, and paths of development in the new world'. *Journal of Economic Perspectives* 14(3): 217–32.

Stein, H. (2008) *Beyond the World Bank Agenda: An institutional ap-*

proach to development. Chicago IL: University of Chicago Press.

Stern, N. (1989) 'The economics of development: a survey'. *The Economic Journal* 99(397): 597–685.

Stiglitz, J. (1996) 'Some lessons from the East Asian miracle'. *World Bank Research Observer* 11(2): 151–77.

Sugihara, K. (2003) 'The East Asian path of economic development: a long-term perspective'. In G. Arrighi, T. Hamashita and M. Selden (eds) *The Resurgence of East Asia: 500, 150 and 50 year perspectives*. London: Routledge, pp. 78–123.

Summers, R. and A. Heston (1991) 'The Penn World Table (Mark 5): an expanded set of international comparisons, 1950–1988'. *Quarterly Journal of Economics* 106(2): 327–68.

Szereszewski, R. (1965) *Structural Changes in the Economy of Ghana, 1891–1911*. London: Weidenfeld and Nicolson.

Taylor, M. (2013) 'Poor numbers: why is Morten Jerven being prevented from presenting his research at UNECA?' *African Arguments*, 19 September. http://africanarguments.org/2013/09/19/poor-numbers-why-is-morten-jerven-being-prevented-from-presenting-his-research-at-uneca-by-magnus-taylor/.

Teferra, D. and J. Knight (2008) *Higher Education in Africa: The international dimension*. Boston MA and Accra: Center for International Higher Education, Lynch School of Education, Boston College and Association of African Universities.

Temple, J. (1998) 'Initial conditions, social capital and growth in zAfrica'. *Journal of African Economies* 7(3): 309–47.

— and P. A. Johnson (1998) 'Social capability and economic growth'. *Quarterly Journal of Economics* 113: 965–90.

Thornton, J. (1992) *Africa and Africans in the Making of the Atlantic World, 1400–1800*. Cambridge: Cambridge University Press.

— (1998) *Africa and Africans in the Making of the Atlantic World, 1400–1800*. 2nd edition. Cambridge: Cambridge University Press.

Tobin, J. (1990) 'The HRAF as a radical text?' *Cultural Anthropology* 5(4): 473–87.

Tosh, J. (1980) 'The cash-crop revolution in tropical agriculture: an agricultural reappraisal'. *African Affairs* 79(314): 79–94.

van de Walle, N. (2001) *African Economies and the Politics of Permanent Crisis, 1979–1999*. Cambridge: Cambridge University Press.

— (2015) 'Africa's development in historical perspective'. *Foreign Affairs*, 22 March 2015. http://www.foreignaffairs.com/articles/143002/edited-by-emmanuel-akyeampong-robert-h-bates-nathan-nunn-and-jam/africas-development-in-historical-perspective.

Vansina, J. (1986) 'Knowledge and perceptions of the African past'. In B. Jewsiewicki and D. Newbury (eds) *African Historiographies: What history for which Africa?* Beverly Hills CA: Sage Publications, pp. 28–41.

Venables, A. (2008) 'Rethinking economic growth in a globalizing world: an economic geography lens'. *African Development Review* 21(2): 331–51.

Wheeler, D. (1984) 'Sources of stagnation in sub-Saharan Africa'. *World Development* 12(1): 1–23.

Woolcock, M., S. Szreter and V. Rao (2009) 'How and why does history matter for development policy?' Policy Research Working Paper 5425. Washington DC: World Bank.

World Bank (1981) *Accelerated Development in Sub-Saharan Africa: An agenda for action*. Washington DC: World Bank. http://documents.worldbank.org/curated/en/1981/01/438047/accelerated-development-sub-saharan-africa-agenda-action.

— (1998) *Proceedings of the World Bank Annual Conference on Development Economics 1998*. Washington DC: World Bank.

— (2002) *World Development Indicators 2002*. Washington DC: International Bank for Reconstruction and Development and World Bank.

— (2007) *World Development Indicators 2007*. Washington DC: International Bank for Reconstruction and Development and World Bank.

— (2012) *World Development Indicators 2012*. Washington DC: International Bank for Reconstruction and Development and World Bank.

— (2014) *World Development Indicators 2014*. Washington DC: International Bank for Reconstruction and Development and World Bank.

York, G. (2013) 'B.C. professor ruffles feathers by spotlighting Africa's data problems'. *The Globe and Mail*, 13 November. http://www.theglobeandmail.com/news/world/bc-professor-ruffles-feathers-by-spotlighting-africas-data-problems/article15434240/.

Young, A. (2012) 'The African growth miracle'. *Journal of Political Economy* 120 (August): 696–739.

Index